SCENES FROM THE PAST

THE RAILWAYS A

PRESTON

An Historical Review

COMPILED and WRITTEN by

GORDON BIDDLE

Copyright © 1989 Foxline Publishing and G. Biddle
ISBN 1 870119 05 3
All rights reserved
Designed and edited by Gregory K. Fox
Printed by Amadeus Press, Huddersfield
Published by Foxline Publishing
32, Urwick Road, Romiley, Stockport.
Re-printed November 1992.

Publisher's Note:
The decision to reprint was taken early in 1992, year of the Preston Guild. It was felt that the event could not be allowed to pass without some recognition, and so with this in mind the book has been extended by the inclusion of an additional eight pages. Items dealt with include traffic arrangements for the 1922 event and the reproduction of a British Railways staff magazine article for 1952.

Preston. 9th August 1956. The route north! This elevated view of the approaches north of Preston station show the dominant features of St. Walburge' Church at the junction of the lines to Blackpool and to Lancaster and Carlisle. Features now gone include the Croft Street mill, which overshadowed Prestor shed, and No.5. signal box perched here at a point marking the end of the Maudland viaduct.

British Rail

Introduction

For centuries Preston's commanding position at the lowest crossing point of the River Ribble, on the narrow stretch of low-lying land between the Pennines and the Irish Sea, has been of strategic importance on the western route from England to Scotland. As Lancashire's oldest borough, not for nothing has the town been known as 'Proud Preston'. From medieval times it was the commercial centre of a large area and an important stopping place on the highway to the north. Daniel Defoe in 1726 called it a fine town full of attorneys, but with no industry. By the end of the century this was changing. In the 1760s Richard Arkwright had produced his spinning frame, and Samuel Horrocks built his first cotton mill in 1791. Although Preston had been a port since at least 1360, it was only in 1806 that a serious effort was made to improve navigation of the Ribble estuary, and Victoria Quay was opened in 1839. Meanwhile the Lancaster Canal connected Preston with Lancaster in 1797, Wigan in 1803 and Kendal in 1819.

By the time the first railway came in 1838, therefore, industry was firmly established and the town no longer was the genteel place it had been. A population of 14,200 in 1801 grew to nearly 53,500 forty years later. From then onwards growth was equally rapid, so that by 1900 there were over 115,000 inhabitants and Preston had assumed the layout and appearance it largely retains today. For this industrialisation the railway can take a large share of the credit or blame, according to one's point of view; suffice to say that the coming of the railway acted as a catalyst for expansion and sustained it for the rest of the century.

Although it was not a railway town in the same sense as Crewe or Swindon, Preston has always been an important junction and for many years the railway was a major employer. Moreover, in contrast to many other railway centres, it has retained its status. Half way between Euston and Glasgow, as both a traffic interchange point and a railhead covering a wide area, Preston today can be considered as the most important intermediate station on the West Coast Main Line, outstripping Crewe. All trains call at Preston, whereas at Crewe this is now far from the case.

Notwithstanding its importance, from early days Preston station had a dreadful reputation among travellers, a situation that did not improve until the 1880s. Even then, despite successive enlargements, at busy periods it continued to form an operating bottleneck until well after the second world war, a feature that can be traced back through an unusual and complex history. The openings of the various lines are shown on the map inside the front cover; closures are given in a table at the back.

Despite contractions in the system, the railway and Preston are still mutually important to each other. Of the eight radiating lines, only two — to Longridge and Southport — have been closed, and although the national decline in freight by rail has affected Preston as much as everywhere else, passenger traffic remains healthy. Indeed, the station itself, now being given a welcome facelift, in many ways has changed little during the last century. The sound of steam beneath the glass roof may have been replaced by the whine of electric locomotives, but our parents and grandparents would still recognise it as the place where they watched the Scotch Express draw in while they waited in the crowd on the opposite platform for a half-day excursion to Blackpool.

This book does not pretend to be a definitive history, and readers wanting to know more are referred to the selected bibliography at the back. However, while it will no doubt evoke memories among older Prestonians it may, I hope, also serve a wider purpose as a record of a rather neglected aspect of the town's history and, perhaps, add a further contribution to understanding the evolution of 'Proud Preston'.

Acknowledgements

A number of people and organisations have assisted with photographs, all of whom are acknowledged in the captions, but I would particularly like to thank Douglas Thompson, Jack Dakres, Richard Casserley (on behalf of H C Casserley), John M Hammond, Norman Parker, R B Holden, J A Coltas, J R Morten and Frank Carpenter of the Harris Museum & Art Gallery, Preston, for their help. Not least, I must also thank my publisher, Greg Fox, for his assistance in tracking down illustrations and genial helpfulness in response to my sometimes impatient requests, and Rex Christiansen for once more readily answering my enquiries.

1950s. Unrebuilt Patriot class engine No 45543 *Home Guard* heads south out of Preston with a London train.   *Photo: British Rail*

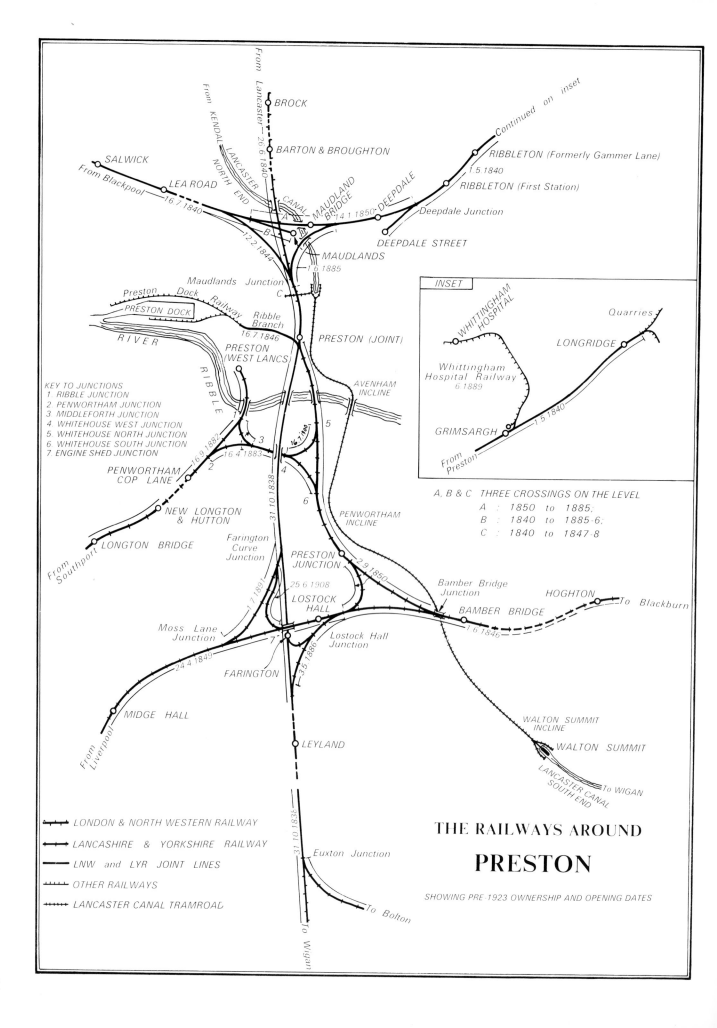

THE RAILWAYS AROUND
PRESTON
SHOWING PRE-1923 OWNERSHIP AND OPENING DATES

: Preston's First Railway: The Old Tramroad

Most Prestonians will know the Old Tram Bridge over the Ribble and the footpath across the fields beyond it called The Old Tramroad, and many may wonder how they acquired their names.

When George and Robert Stephenson engineered the Stockton & Darlington Railway that marked the beginning of the railway era, they were not inventing something new but were refining an old concept, for the principle of a wheeled vehicle running on a fixed track goes back to ancient times. In seventeenth century Britain primitive wooden horse-drawn waggonways were being built to connect mines to navigable rivers and, later, canals. Wooden rails were superseded by iron, some with a flat surface on which flanged wheels could run, as on a modern railway, and others, called tramroads or plateways, having flanged rails for use with flat-wheeled wagons. One such was the tramroad built — rather unusually — to connect the two isolated portions of the Lancaster Canal at Preston.

The canal was planned to run from Westhoughton, near Wigan, to Kendal in order to take coal northward and bring south the limestone that was quarried in Westmorland and North Lancashire, for use in iron smelting and for calcining into lime for agricultural and building purposes. The two main natural obstacles were the Ribble and the Lune. Because Lancaster and Kendal interests predominated among the canal company shareholders, the River Lune was bridged first, by the impressive aqueduct at Lancaster. By 1799 the canal had been completed between Wigan and a point north of Chorley, and from Preston through Lancaster to a point north of Carnforth, leaving a gap in the middle. By this time the company had exhausted its capital, so as a temporary expedient to get through traffic moving and produce revenue, a tramroad was laid to connect the North and South Ends of the canal, as they became officially known, until locks and an aqueduct could be built across the valley. The South End was therefore extended a few more miles to Walton Summit, at the edge of the escarpment overlooking the Ribble, and the two sections of canal were joined by rails in 1803. In 1819 the North End reached Kendal, but the vital connecting link at Preston was never built and the tramroad became permanent.

With the exception of a section through a short tunnel under Fishergate, the tramroad had double track throughout, laid on roughly squared stone sleeper blocks, and trains comprised up to six wagons drawn by horses. At three places steep changes in level were overcome by constructing inclines where wagons were raised and lowered by attaching them to an endless chain running round large wheels at top and bottom and operated by a stationary steam engine.

1. Preston, Canal Basin c.1923. A barge being worked under the lift bridge used for transferring coal wagons from one side to the other.
Photo: Author's collection

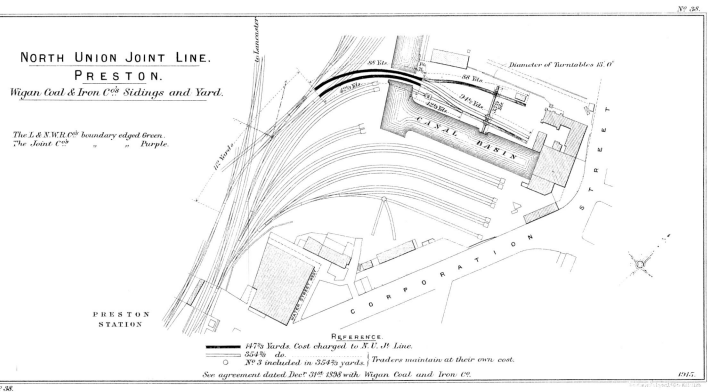

NORTH UNION JOINT LINE.
PRESTON.
Wigan Coal & Iron Cºs Sidings and Yard.

The L & N.W.R. Cºs boundary edged Green.
The Joint Cºs   „   „   Purple.

PRESTON
STATION

REFERENCE.
147⅔ Yards. Cost charged to N.U. Jt Line.
354⅔   do.
o   Nº 3 included in 354⅔ yards. } *Traders maintain at their own cost.*
See agreement dated Decr 31st 1898 with Wigan Coal and Iron Cº.

At Preston the line began at the canal basin close to Corporation Street where Ladywell House now stands, and ran beneath Fishergate and across the bottom of Garden Street into what is now Avenham Park. The present tunnel leading to the Asda car park is an enlargement of the original, and what may be a stone bridge abutment still exists in Garden Street. The steepest incline was at Avenham, descending at 1 in 6 on to a wooden bridge over the river — the Old Tram Bridge — with the winding engine house at the top. The present concrete bridge is very similar in outline to the original. The tramroad then crossed the meadows beyond on a low embankment — now a footpath — to the next incline close to Carr Wood. Named the Penwortham Incline, it was taken out of use about 1820 when the line was diverted on to an easier gradient capable of being used by horses. Thence the line ran across Watering Pool Lane and Todd Lane, as far as which it is still a footpath, to Bamber Bridge, from where on most of it has been obliterated by building development.

After crossing Station Road in Bamber Bridge the tramroad ran across fields to cross Kellet Lane and Gough Lane, where a very short length still remains in the midst of the new trading estate, and then ascended the third incline to the South End of the canal at Walton Summit, from which the area takes its name. The Walton Incline engine house was at the bottom, which with an endless chain was, of course, quite feasible. At the top were three large canal basins and a transhipment shed, but now the entire site has been covered by new roads, the M61 and housing, as part of the Central Lancashire New Town project. However, it was a happy thought to name one of the roads Tramway Lane, but less so with Outram Way at Bamber Bridge which perpetuates the myth that Benjamin Outram was the engineer. Although he was an outstanding 18th century canal engineer who also built numerous tramroads, it was in fact his contemporary, William Jessop, an equally noted engineer, who was called in to approve the plans for the Preston and Walton Summit tramroad. The man who actually designed it and supervised construction was the canal company's resident engineer, William Cartwright.

In 1837 the canal company leased the tramroad to the newly formed Bolton & Preston Railway company which wanted to use the route as a way into Preston. In the event they chose to do so over the North Union Railway from a junction at Euxton and therefore had no use for the tramroad, but under the terms of the lease were compelled to maintain it for the canal company's traffic, which they and their successors went on doing until 1864 when the canal itself was leased — the South End to the Leeds & Liverpool Canal company (with which it connected at Wigan and Wheelton) and the North End, together with the tramroad, to the London & North Western Railway.

After the railway from the south was opened, carriers on the canal found it quicker and cheaper to move coal from the Wigan pits to

Preston by rail, where transhipment sidings were built alongside the canal basin. Although there was still some traffic on the tramroad between the Summit and Bamber Bridge, by 1864 the section onward to Preston had for some years been little used. The new owner promptly closed it north of Bamber Bridge; the portion from there t Walton Summit remained open to 1879. Traffic continued on the Nort End of the canal until 1947, in latter days mainly comprising coal, sinc when the section in Preston south of Aqueduct Street has progressivel been filled in so that few traces now remain.

2. Preston, Canal Basin c.1923. The one that got away; a Wigan Coal & Iro Company's wagon that tipped too far. *Photo: Author's collectio*

3. Preston, Canal Basin, 1960. A wagon tippler on to which wagons wer swivelled by a turntable for loading coal into barges. Note County Hall in the lef background, one of the remaining landmarks that can identify the location.
Photo: J. Parkinso

5. (Right) Old Tram Bridge. Horses and wagons crossing the bridge in Thomas Lynch's painting *View of Avenham Park c 1862.* Despite artist's licence in the location of the engine house chimney on the left and Hoghton Tower in the distance, it gives a good impression of the overall view.
Photo: Author's collection courtesy Harris Museum

6. (Right—second from top) Old Tram Bridge, 1860's. The bridge showing the bottom of the incline and lower winding drum. *Photo: Author's collection*

7. (Right—third from top) Nr. Brownedge, March 1971. A low embankment marks the tramroad's course near Todd Lane, still unchanged, albeit for encroaching vegetation, today. *Photo: Author*

4. (Below) Avenham Incline. The engine house at the top, after it was closed in 1864 but before demolition in 1869. The setts were laid for walking the tram horses up and down; part of the winding frame and tram rails can be seen on the far left. *Photo: Harris Museum*

OLD TRAM BRIDGE

8. (Right—bottom) Walton Summit, April 1959. This former weighbridge house alongside the tramroad adjacent to Gough Lane is now the only remaining relic in this area. *Photo: Author*

9. (Left) Summit Farm, April 1953. Looking up Walton Summit Incline from Summit Farm, showing stone sleeper blocks re-laid to form a farm cart road. The site has now completely disappeared. *Photo: Author*

10. (Right) Summit, April 1953. The disused canal basins at the Summit, showing the middle wall of the former trans-shipment shed in the centre. Tramroad rails ran along the sides of the basins. *Photo: Author*

11. (Left) Nr. Todd Lane, March 1971. A row of stone sleeper blocks still in place near Todd Lane. The holes held spikes securing the rails. *Photo: Author*

12. (Right) Brownedge, March 1971. A section of tramroad rail from Fishergate tunnel, used on an allotment at Brownedge. *Photo: Author*

3. Preston, c.1953. LMS "Duchess" No 46237 *City of Bristol* pulls away from the station past No 1 Signal box with an up Scottish express. Premier train on the Euston to Glasgow route was the Royal Scot with a journey time of eight hours.

Photo: Eric Treacy

: The Main Lines

The first railway proper to reach Preston was the North Union Railway, entering from the south in 1838 and immediately opening up rail communication with London, Birmingham, Liverpool and Manchester. Commencing north of Warrington, it formed junctions with the Liverpool & Manchester Railway at Newton and in 1843 the Bolton & Preston Railway joined it at Euxton Junction to form a new direct route to Preston from Manchester, followed in 1849 by the East Lancashire Railway's direct line from Liverpool via Ormskirk. Extension northward was made progressively by the Lancaster & Preston Junction Railway, opened in 1840, the Lancaster & Carlisle Railway in 1846 and the Caledonian Railway from the border city to Edinburgh and Glasgow in 1848.

With its headquarters at Preston, the North Union was thus a vital link in the chain, a situation it was not slow to exploit by trying to impose exorbitant financial terms on its neighbours for the use of its line and station at Preston, without which through services from London to Scotland could not be properly established. The North Union built its station on the south side of Fishergate. The Lancaster line stopped short of Fishergate, near the canal basin, and the North Union undertook to build a connecting line through a short tunnel to give the Lancaster & Preston Railway access to its station in return for a contribution towards the cost. A year after the Lancaster line was opened the North Union gave what in effect was six months' notice to quit, whereupon the Lancaster company turned to the Bolton & Preston Railway for help. The latter was not yet complete and, despite having abandoned its intention of using the course of the canal tramroad as a route into Preston, was still pressing on with a scheme for its own station on the north side of Fishergate on a site occupied by Maxwell House behind the Victoria Hotel. Although unfinished, the station was hastily made ready to receive the Lancaster trains.

This arrangement was of no use for through services of course, where there was no choice but to use the North Union's station, for which that company demanded a heavy toll for trains passing over the connecting line through the tunnel. Having paid part of the cost of making it, the Lancaster & Preston naturally refused, whereupon the North Union rejected through bookings and imposed a toll of 6d (2½p) per head on

14. (Left) Walton Summit, April 1968. A North Union relic: an iron boundary post at Walton Summit canal basin, into whose ownership the canal passed from the Bolton and Preston Railway. The pattern of the boundary post was more commonly associated with the London and North Western Railway, which became a partner in the North Union. *Photo: Author*

15. (Below). Stone sleeper blocks and a section of North Union rail removed from the Ribble Branch, but similar to early main line permanent way.
Photo: J. M. Dakres

individual passengers instead. Being in possession of a through ticket, most passengers objected to paying extra for such a short distance, preferring to get out and walk from one station to the other while the carriages were taken through the tunnel, only to find as often as not that, in the southbound direction, the North Union had deliberately despatched the train without them.

Simultaneously the Lancaster Canal company, which had opposed the railway from the outset, was making strenuous efforts to retain its traffic from Preston to Lancaster and Kendal. Since the opening of the North Union Railway it had run an efficient and lucrative service of swift passenger boats that connected with the trains at Preston, which the opening of the line onwards to Lancaster had forced it to discontinue as far as that point, and it could foresee the day when its goods traffic would be similarly affected. Beset by the obstructive attitude of the North Union on one hand and cut-throat competition from the canal on the other, by 1842 the Lancaster & Preston's finances were in such a desperate state that it was driven to the extraordinary course of leasing its line to the canal at an annual rental. The canal company immediately took over and from September 1842 operated the trains for the next six years, making a handsome profit from them into the bargain, albeit by removing the seats from third class carriages so that more passengers could be accommodated standing up.

Then in 1846 the Lancaster & Carlisle Railway entered the scene. It was a much more powerful company than the little Lancaster & Preston Railway, over which it proceeded to ride roughshod by insisting on running its own trains to and from Carlisle over the Lancaster & Preston instead of handing them over at Lancaster. The canal company's protests were ignored on the grounds that the lease was not legally binding — which was true, for it had been imperfectly drawn up

and the Lancaster & Carlisle discovered the loophole. So from 1846 1848 there existed the ludicrous and highly dangerous situation of t canal company running the local trains and the Lancaster & Carli independently running the through expresses on a line over which the respective legal rights at best were questionable. The actual owners, t Lancaster & Preston company, by this time were quite powerless; t board of directors had resigned en bloc and the shareholders had means of appointing a new one.

Inevitably there was an accident. A Lancaster & Carlisle express r into the back of a Lancaster & Preston stopping train at Bay Hor station and the Board of Trade stepped in to enforce some sort of orde with the result that the canal company relinquished its lease in favour the Lancaster & Carlisle. In the meantime the North Union had be leased jointly by larger companies that later became part of t Lancashire & Yorkshire and London & North Western Railways, a thereafter relative peace reigned at Preston.

The line to Blackpool started life as the Preston & Wyre Railway Harbour Company. It opened the line from Preston to Fleetwood a fe weeks after the Lancaster line in 1840 and had its own station Leighton Street called Maudlands, to reach which it crossed t Lancaster line on the level. There was also a connecting curve in t southward direction. Until completion of the rail route to Scotland t line formed the quickest way of getting from London to Glasgow, means of a connecting steamer service from the new port of Fleetwoc to Ardrossan. Branches from Kirkham to Lytham and from Poulton Blackpool were opened in 1846, the latter soon becoming much t most important line in the Fylde so far as passenger traffic w concerned. The Preston & Wyre was taken over jointly by the Londo & North Western and Lancashire & Yorkshire Railways in 1849.

16. North Union Bridge, 1870s. The first main line bridge over the Ribble was completed in 1838 by the engineer Charles Vignoles, and successively widened in 1879 an 1904. Beyond can be seen the original East Lancashire Bridge, and part of the viaduct that was replaced by an embankment in 1884-86. *Photo: Harris Museu*

No. 17. (above) Euxton. April 1929. The "Coronation Scot" streamlined express in the special blue and silver livery design of this train, approaches Euxton on its journey south, hauled by "Princess Coronation" Class 4-6-2 No. **6220** *Coronation*, temporarily disguised as No. **6229** *Duchess of Hamilton*, which had been shipped to the United States of America in January 1939 to represent British railways at the New York World Fair. In its streamlined state, the locomotive carried an electric headlight and bell for operation on American railroads. Moments of glory continue for Duchess of Hamilton with its preservation, albeit in modified form, at the National Railway Museum.

E.R. Morten.

18. (Centre) Leyland, c.1920. A Lancashire and Yorkshire Railway "High Flyer", 4-4-2 No 1394, speeds past Euxton Coal Siding signal box, south of Leyland, with a Manchester to Blackpool express. Motive power and rolling stock on the route was varied but the signal box remained unchanged over the years until closure on 14th November 1965.
Photo: H. Gordon Tidey/Real Photographs

19. Leyland, December 1964. In this view looking north towards Preston, the original North Union buildings are to the left of the picture. The structures on the island and right hand platforms are of LNWR origin, an early variation of a standard adopted by the company. The small goods yard, situated on the far side of the road overbridge, was closed on 25th November 1968. The line was quadrupled between Euxton and Preston between 1889 and 1891 to accommodate the enormous growth of traffic. *Photo: Author*

20. (Above) Farington, c.1920. A London and North Western Aberdeen express headed by "Prince of Wales" Class 4-6-0 No 1478 is seen north of the station. Coote Lane overbridge can be seen in the background.

Photo: H. Gordon Tidey/Real Photographs

21. (Centre) Farington, May 1954. The entrance may have been insignificant but there was no doubt about its location!

Photo: Author

22. (Below) Farington, April 1957. This view, taken from the down slow platform, shows the all-timber construction of the station buildings so characteristic of the LNWR. Looking south, Farington Junction signal box is just visible through the bridge opening. Although it was to close some three years later, Farington had quite a healthy service with twenty or so southbound trains calling during weekdays, mainly locals to Manchester or Leyland but the odd one to Wigan and Crewe.

Photo: H. C. Casserley

Farington, c.1920. The mainstays of LNWR heavy freight trains were their 0-8-0 goods engines. No 2117 is here leaving Farington Curve Junction southbound, with Flag Lane Bridge in the distance.
Photo: LGRP/courtesy David & Charles

(Centre) Farington, c.1964. With a train of empty mineral wagons, Class 5 4-6-0 No 45082 eases past Farington Junction on its way south. The rear of the train is just passing the 90 lever signal box of 1910, which in turn had replaced a twenty eight year old structure erected for the quadrupling. Above the locomotive can be seen the coaling plant of Lostock Hall engine shed. Trains coming from the East Lancashire line were required to observe a miles per hour speed limit round the sharp curve. *Photo: S. Withers*

Farington, July 1965. A view from Bee Lane bridge as BR "Britannia" class 4-6-2 No 70003 *John Bunyan* approaches Farington Curve Junction on a Carlisle-Crewe parcels train. *Photo: John M. Hammond*

26. Preston, March 1964. Rebuilt "Patriot" Class 4-6-0 No 45512 *Bunsen* of Upperby (Carlisle) shed, enters the station with a nine coach relief train from Crewe to Glasgow. The reporting number 1S99 indicates that the working is for a class 'A'-express-train travelling between England and Scotland, hence the letter 'S', although on this occasion the number 99 gives rise to the belief that it is an extra to the scheduled relief trains and would be at relatively short notice.

Photo: M. S. Welch

27. Preston, May 1957. Crisp early evening shadows spread over "Jubilee" Class 6P 4-6-0 No 45671 *Prince Rupert* as the 4.10pm Manchester to Blackpool Nort awaits departure from platform 3. This Newton Heath engine was a regular performer on the route. The particular working ran non stop to Bolton and then stopped a Chorley and Leyland before arrival in Preston at 5.2pm. An eight minute stay was followed by calls at Salwick, Kirkham, Poulton and Layton before arrival in th seaside town at 5.47pm.

Photo: T. Lew

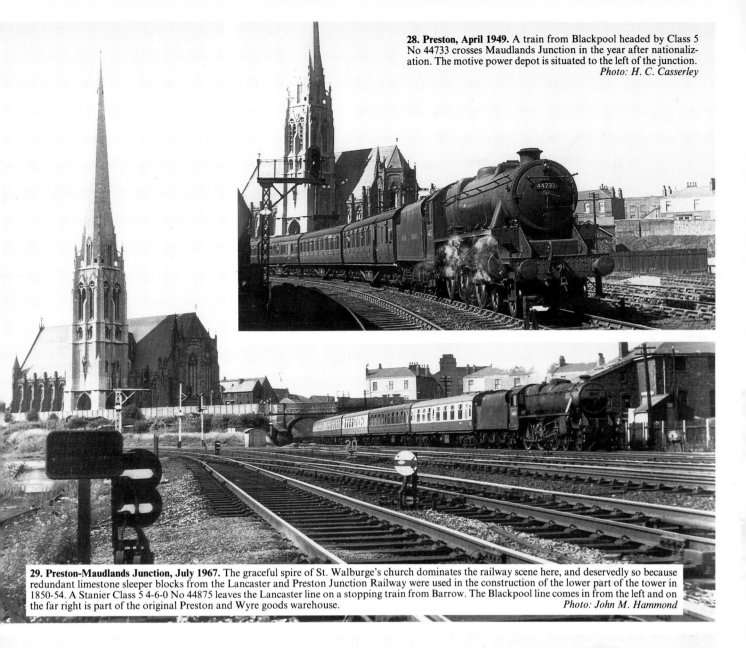

28. Preston, April 1949. A train from Blackpool headed by Class 5 No 44733 crosses Maudlands Junction in the year after nationalization. The motive power depot is situated to the left of the junction.
Photo: H. C. Casserley

29. Preston-Maudlands Junction, July 1967. The graceful spire of St. Walburge's church dominates the railway scene here, and deservedly so because redundant limestone sleeper blocks from the Lancaster and Preston Junction Railway were used in the construction of the lower part of the tower in 1850-54. A Stanier Class 5 4-6-0 No 44875 leaves the Lancaster line on a stopping train from Barrow. The Blackpool line comes in from the left and on the far right is part of the original Preston and Wyre goods warehouse.
Photo: John M. Hammond

30. Oxheys Sidings, 1966. British Railways Standard Class 6MT 4-6-0 No 72001 *Clan Cameron* accelerates beneath Blackpool Road bridge on its way north. Oxheys was the location for sidings serving Preston corporation cattle market, which closed two years later as cattle traffic transferred to road.
Photo: B. Reynolds

31. (Left) Barton and Broughton, c.1959. Fo
miles north of Preston was this small statie
serving a rural community. The main buil
ings, to the left in this view towards Lancaste
were built by the Lancaster & Preston Railwa
and still stand. The utilitarian timber buildin
on the up side reflected the expectations of t
LNWR when providing fairly limited passe
ger accommodation and were a variation of t
"portable huts" to be found throughout t
system. *Photo: G. H. Pla*

32. (Centre) Brock, early 1930's. A "Roy
Scot" class locomotive approaches the statie
with a southbound stopping train. This sma
station, situated 7 miles from Preston, serve
the nearby farming community. Like Barton,
had an original Lancaster & Preston sto
building with LNWR wooden additions, a
was an early victim of road competitio
closing in 1939. *Photo: D. Thompse*

33. (Below) Brock, 1920's. An old LNW
locomotive, "Samson" class 2-4-0, former
No 737 *Roberts*, and dating from 1864-6
hauls the District Engineer's inspection saloo
over the water troughs north of Brock. T
engine, named *Engineer Lancaster* was, as i
title implied, for use by that department an
followed a tradition of using similar engin
for work with other district engineerir
organizations on the LNWR, and for a time o
the LMSR afterwards.
Photo: H. Gordon Tidey/Real Photograp

34. (Below-left) Brock, 24th June 1932.
former LNWR "Prince of Wales" class 4-6
No 5634 *William Cowper*, takes a Windermer
train over Brock water troughs beneath one
the two ornamental bridges built for t
Brockholes family of Claughton Hall an
bearing their badger emblem.
Photo: E. R. Morte

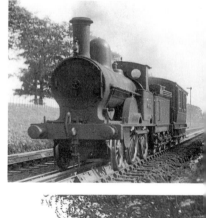

35. Salwick, c.1930's. The first two stations on the quadrupled section of the Blackpool line, Lea Road and Salwick, were completed to an almost identical design save for the fact that the former was served from a nearby underbridge and Salwick was reached by inclined ramp from an overbridge. The island platforms were situated between the slow lines, an operating feature favoured by the Lancashire and Yorkshire Railway, which was responsible for the Preston & Wyre joint line. Once again, these two stations served agricultural areas and saw little in the way of local patronage. Lea Road subsequently closed in 1938 but Salwick survives to serve nearby industrial premises with a handful of trains stopping at peak times.
Photo: D. Thompson

36. Lea Road, 1966. A "Patriot" class locomotive on a Blackpool train heads through the closed station shortly before demolition began. The design of platform buildings, with cast iron columns and brackets, was very robust, and repeated widely throughout the LYR system. Although subject to minor variations, it was a recognisable style typical of the solid construction techniques of the period.
Photo: R. B. Holden

37. Lea Road, April 1939. A Blackpool bound train, headed by LMS No 10412, speeds along the fast line west of Lea Road station. This quadrupled section between Preston and Kirkham created improved methods of handling the large volumes of traffic to and from the Fylde coast. Rationalization in the Blackpool area in 1964 resulted in the cutting back of line capacity, the fast lines between Kirkham and Maudlands being taken out of use from the 14th November 1965.
Photo: E. R. Morten

38. Longridge, c.1914. This view towa[rds]
Preston shows the long platform cano[py]
almost a case of over provision when [one]
considers the comparatively short life [of]
the passenger train service.
Photo: Norman Parker collect[ion]

39. Preston–Deepdale Street, May 19[??].
The original Preston and Longri[dge]
stations were quite primitive, perman[ent]
buildings not being erected until after [the]
company was taken over. The stati[on]
building at the original Preston termin[us]
seen here, bears the date 1850 but has n[ow]
been demolished. Passenger servi[ce]
ceased as early as 1856, but the yard is s[till]
used for goods. *Photo: Auth[or]*

3: The Longridge Branch

In the early 19th century the quarries on the fell above Longridge were
finding difficulty in meeting the demand for their stone, mainly because
of inadequate transport. Many prominent buildings in Preston are
constructed in it, while the Liverpool docks, Fleetwood docks and sea
defence works on the Fylde coast all used Longridge Fell stone.

In 1836 the Preston & Longridge Railway company was incor-
porated by Act of Parliament to build a line 6½ miles long from the
quarries to Preston. The chairman was Peter Hesketh Fleetwood, MP
for Preston, and the single line railway was opened to a terminus in
Deepdale Street in 1840. Until 1848 it was worked entirely by horses,
wagons descending the steep section from the quarries to Longridge
station by gravity, with the horses that had taken them up riding in a
van. On Wednesdays and Saturdays two passenger trains ran each way,
also horse-drawn.

Intermittently during the last century the Preston & Longridge was
seen as a key element in a number of ambitious schemes for cross-
country railways linking Fleetwood and Preston with Yorkshire and
the north east, only the first of which actually constructed anything, and
a very short line at that. Its grand title was the Fleetwood Preston &
West Riding Junction Railway, and it proposed to build a short link
from the Preston & Wyre Railway's terminus at Maudlands, referred to
in the last chapter, to the Preston & Longridge line near Deepdale
Street, which would then be widened as far as Grimsargh whence a new
line was projected to run through Clitheroe to a point near Skipton
where access would be gained to railways in Yorkshire.

In the event, apart from a curiously isolated excavation near Hurst
Green, which can still be seen, the only work completed was the 1½
miles of double track at the Preston end. Opened in 1850, it left the
Preston & Wyre line near Pedder Street, crossed the main line to the
north on the level, and shortly beyond a bridge over the canal plunged
into a tunnel 862 yd long to emerge just short of St Pauls Road. It then
passed beneath Deepdale Road and joined the original Longridge line a
short distance out from the terminus at what became known as
Deepdale Junction. The tunnel in fact is broken into three sections by
short lengths of open cutting which are hidden behind the backs of
houses and factories.

Meanwhile the new company had leased the Preston & Longridge,
only to default in paying the rent so that the latter regained possession
in 1852. Four years later the FP&WRJ company underwent a financial
reorganisation and obtained a second Act empowering it to purchase
the Longridge line, which it did by instalments from 1856. A primitive
station was opened adjoining the canal bridge, called Maudland Bridge,
and another in Deepdale Road called Deepdale Bridge. The latter
replaced the original terminus which then became a goods depot. In
1866 the line was acquired jointly by the London & North Western and
Lancashire & Yorkshire Railways, although even then there was no
direct access to the main station at Preston until 1885 when the present
curve was opened and Maudland Bridge, together with the level
crossing over the main line, was closed.

In 1889 a private branch off the Longridge line was opened from
Grimsargh for nearly two miles to the mental hospital at Whittingham,

40. Preston–Deepdale, June 1953. The station in Deepdale Road, opened by th[e]
Fleetwood, Preston and West Riding Junction Railway, was still largely inta[ct]
some 23 years after closure. The building housed the company offices but ha[s]
since been demolished. *Photo: Autho[r]*

mainly for carrying coal and stores. From the outset a free passenge[r]
service was operated for staff and visitors. Nine trains a day connecte[d]
with Preston and Longridge trains at Grimsargh, where the hospita[l]
railway had a separate station on the opposite side of the level crossing[.]
The Whittingham terminus was quite impressive, with a glass roo[f]
beyond which the line continued to sidings and the hospital boile[r]
house.

Passenger services between Preston and Longridge were an earl[y]
casualty to road transport, ceasing in 1930, but the County Council'[s]
hospital trains continued to run until 1957, connecting with buses a[t]
Grimsargh. In later years the hospital passenger coaches comprise[d]

(continued on next page[)]

42. Preston–Ribbleton, May 1954. The original station was open for only three years from 1863, thereafter being occasionally used for Fulwood Barracks, situated nearby. The platform, however, lasted for many years. *Photo: Author*

41. Preston–Deepdale, June 1953. The entrance to the station was by this small building on the adjacent road overbridge. For many years it saw use as a shop but has since, inevitably, been demolished. *Photo: Author*

43. Preston–Ribbleton, June 1952. Gammull Lane station, opened in 1854, spelt Gammer Lane – local pronunciation being taken literally? – and renamed Fulwood in 1856. It was finally renamed Ribbleton in 1900. *Photo: Author*

(continued from previous page)

three converted goods brake vans fitted with benches along the sides. Goods trains went on running to Longridge up to 1967, although the last train ran on 5 May 1968 when an engine went up to Longridge to collect an empty wagon that had taken a load of ashes to repair a railway footpath. Regular stone traffic from Longridge had transferred to road soon after the 1914-18 war, although the track into the quarries remained until 1940. After closure the line to Longridge was lifted beyond Courtaulds' Red Scar Works sidings. Opened in 1938, Courtaulds had two Peckett 0-4-0 saddle tank engines, replaced for the last few years by a Sentinel diesel. After the closure of the factory this section in turn was closed in 1980 and dismantled beyond a point just south of Blackpool Road. Paradoxically, the original Preston terminus in Deepdale Street is still in use as a coal and oil terminal, reached by reversing trains at Deepdale Junction.

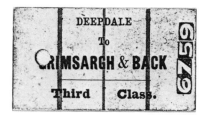

DEEPDALE
To
GRIMSARGH & BACK
Third · Class.
6759

44. Grimsargh, May 1954. This view towards Longridge shows the single storey stone building which latterly housed facilities for parcels and goods traffic, regular passenger trains having ceased as long ago as 1930. *Photo: Author*

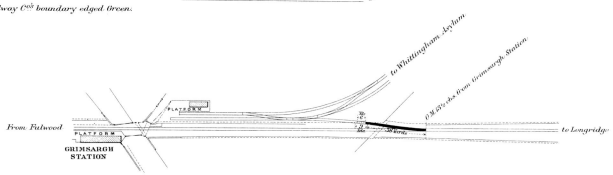

PRESTON AND LONGRIDGE LINE.
GRIMSARGH.
Whittingham Lunatic Asylum, Siding.

The Joint Railway Cº's boundary edged Green.

PLATFORM

PLATFORM
GRIMSARGH
STATION

From Fulwood

to Whittingham Asylum

0 M. 15½ chs from Grimsargh Station

to Longridge

REFERENCE.

38 Yards maintained by L & N.W.R.Cº on Joint land at Committee's cost.
15   do   do   do   do   on Private land at   do

Agreement dated 22ⁿᵈ May 1892 with Committee of Whittingham Lunatic Asylum.

L. 1916.

45. Grimsargh, May 1954. The Grimsargh terminus of the Whittingham Hospital Railway, alongside the Longridge branch on the left and just across the road from the "main line" station. *Photo: Author*

46. Grimsargh, June 1952. From 1947 to 1956, the Whittingham trains were worked by a former London, Brighton and South Coast Railway 0-6-2 tank engine built in 1886, purchased second hand and named *James Fryars* after a hospital chairman. Here, it leaves Grimsargh with a passenger train consisting of converted goods brake vans. *Photo: Author*

47. Grimsargh, April 1957. The last engine used on the Whittingham line was a vertical boilered Sentinel named *Gradwell*, seen here at Grimsargh with Driver Wright and Fireman Bennett.

Photo: Norman Jones

48. Grimsargh, 6th April 1957. Driver G. Wright, who has spent his working life driving on the Whittingham Hospital Railway stands alongside *Gradwell*, the Sentinel steam shunter. Every Saturday, for nearly half a century, he and his mate have worked 18 booked passenger trains over the two mile single line from Grimsargh and on this occasion it is the 1.30pm Saturdays Only. The passenger coach is converted from an LNWR goods brake van. Since opening in 1889 the line had owned four locomotives, two of which, 0-4-0 tanks, were built by Barclays. A third engine, London, Brighton and South Coast Railway 0-4-2 tank designed by William Stroudley, was second hand. The fourth and sole surviving motive power is the Sentinel vehicle seen here. Some weeks later, Driver Wright was to open the regulator for the last time, when, following the 7.20pm run from Grimsargh to Whittingham, the line closed.

Photo: Norman Jones

49. Whittingham Hospital, April 1957. Built on a curve, with a glass overall roof, the station was curiously elaborate for so small a line. *Photo: Norman Jones*

50. Whittingham Hospital, April 1957. *Gradwell* propels its train out of the station towards Grimsargh

Photo: Norman Jone

51. Whittingham Hospital, April 1957. Beyond the station the line ran on through the hospital grounds to the boiler house and sidings. Here *Gradwell* takes a coal wago
past the ornamental pond

Photo: Norman Jone

52. (Above-left) Longridge, c.1910. Somewhat curiously, the station was built on to the Towneley Arms Hotel. The LNWR push-and-pull train with a Webb 2-4-2 tank engine in the middle worked the branch for a short period at this time. *Photo: Norman Parker collection*

55. (Above) Longridge, c.1959. The mini-signal box at Longridge. *Photo: G. H. Platt*

53. (Left) Longridge, May 1954. A later scene at Longridge as Fowler 2-6-4 tank No 42316 draws in with a special Stephenson Locomotive Society railtour of lines closed to passengers in North Lancashire. This special train left Preston at 2.15pm, running immediately to Longridge before returning for a trip up the West Coast main line to Garstang and the remaining section of the Knott End line, closed beyond Pilling. Journeying then via the Glasson Dock branch, Arnside, Sandside, Hincaster Junction and Lancaster, the tour was due to arrive back at Preston at 9pm, having completed a distance of some 123 miles for a bargain eighteen shillings (90p). *Photo: Author*

54. Longridge, c.1959. Beyond Berry Lane level crossing, the line continued towards Tootal Heights quarries. Goods facilities were finally withdrawn in 1967 although from an official point of view, the notice issued by the signal and telegraph department simply commented that *the single line from Deepdale Junction signal box has been severed at a point 350 yards on the Longridge side of Courtaulds No 2 ground frame.* *Photo: G. H. Platt*

56. Longridge, c.1920's. A view looking down Berry Lane showing level crossing gates and the small signal box. The Towneley Arms is behind.

Photo: Norman Parker collection

57. Grimsargh, May 1954. A joint lin trespass notice, reminder of the P&L later owners. *Photo: Autho*

58. (Left) Longridge, October 1969. The abandoned tunnel into the quarries at Longridge. The keystone is dated 1839 and bears the initials PLR and those of the chairman, Peter Hesketh Fleetwood – FHP – back to front. *Photo: Author*

59. (Right) Deepdale, February 1973. This more permanent record marks the boundary of the joint line's property on the pavement at the corner of Deepdale Road and Burrows Road, Preston, and can still be seen. *Photo: Author*

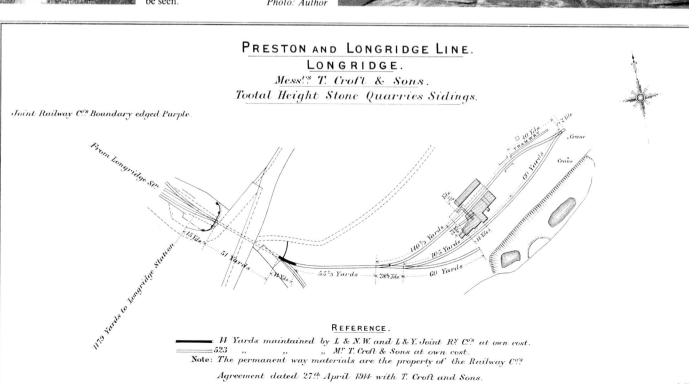

N.º 47.

PRESTON AND LONGRIDGE LINE.

LONGRIDGE.

Mess.ʳˢ T. Croft & Sons.

Tootal Height Stone Quarries Sidings.

Joint Railway Cᵒ.ˢ Boundary edged Purple.

From Longridge Stn.

179 Yards to Longridge Station

TRAMWAY

15 Yds.

51 Yards

11 Yds.

55⅔ Yards

28½ Yds.

60 Yards

105 Yards

110⅔ Yards

60 Yards

Crane

Crane

REFERENCE.

14 Yards maintained by L & N.W. and L & Y. Joint Rᵞ Cᵒ.ˢ at own cost.

523 „ „ „ Mʳ T. Croft & Sons at own cost.

Note: *The permanent way materials are the property of the Railway Cᵒ.ˢ*

Agreement dated 27.ᵗʰ April 1914 with T. Croft and Sons.

N.º 47.

L 1916.

60. East Lancashire Bridge, pre-1869. The original iron bridge across the Ribble on the East Lancashire "Extension", which also carried a public footway at the insistence of Preston Corporation, and was perpetuated in the replacement steel girder bridge of 1930. Avenham Incline chimney can be seen in the distance.

Photo: Harris Museum

East Lancashire and Liverpool

Rail connections east of Preston began with the opening of the Blackburn & Preston Railway in 1846. It joined the North Union by a sharply curved junction immediately south of Farington station. A little over two months later the company was taken over by the East Lancashire Railway, which then proceeded to acquire the Liverpool Ormskirk & Preston Railway on which construction had yet to start. It was completed in 1849 and crossed the North Union north of Farington to join the Blackburn line at Lostock Hall, where trains from Liverpool had to reverse to reach Preston. This awkward arrangement lasted until the following year when the East Lancashire gained independent access to Preston station over its 'Preston Extension' line from a triangular junction between Lostock Hall and Bamber Bridge, involving a 52-arch viaduct across the valley and a third rail bridge over the Ribble, lying between the North Union's and the Old Tram Bridge. The curve to Farington was closed, although in 1886 part was used for a new south-facing junction with the North Union that allowed goods trains to run direct from Blackburn towards Wigan.

Entry into Preston from Liverpool was still rather roundabout, however, and remained so until 1891 when the Lancashire & Yorkshire Railway, with which the East Lancashire had amalgamated, opened a more direct line between Moss Lane Junction and Farington Curve Junction (which was not the same as the earlier Farington curve further south) on the North Union north of Farington station. The complex layout in this area was completed in 1908 when another curve, from Lostock Hall Engine Shed Junction, provided a second route into Preston from the east Lancashire direction, enabling Blackpool trains to run into the west side of Preston station without blocking the main line and causing delay to north-south expresses at busy times (see map).

This is now the only route from east Lancashire, as the Extension line, together with the direct east-west link between Lostock Hall and Moss Lane Junction, was closed in 1972. Although the line to Liverpool is still open there are no through trains any longer. It has been singled to Ormskirk, where only an emergency connection has been retained and passengers have to change to the Merseyrail electrics. Usually it is quicker to travel by the advertised route through Wigan.

61. Todd Lane Junction, c.1960. Originally named Preston Junction, it not only caused confusion with Preston itself but was badly chosen because passengers changed trains there into trains *from* Preston. Changes *for* Preston were made at Lostock Hall. Nevertheless the name was kept for a century until 1952 when the station, but not the signal box, was renamed Todd Lane Junction. Here an eastbound hopper wagon train passes through headed by ex-War Department 2-10-0 locomotive 90471.

Photo: B. Reynolds

62. (Above) Bamber Bridge, c.1959. Many a holiday maker will have cursed the level crossing at Bamber bridge in the days before the Preston by-pass. This view catches the departure of an eastbound Cravens dmu. Of interest in the foreground is the glazed roofing of the subway, quite a novel feature so near to a level crossing. *Photo: G. H. Platt*

63. (Above-right) Bamber Bridge, May 1954. View looking east, showing in the centre the original East Lancashire Railway building and low platform, and the unusual flat-roofed signal box. *Photo: Author*

64. Bamber Bridge, c.1959. Eastbound trains stopped adjacent to this small stone built waiting room, added to the original station by the LYR, perhaps somewhat grimy but containing all the basic facilities which were taken for granted yet soon to be a thing of the past. *Photo: G. H. Platt*

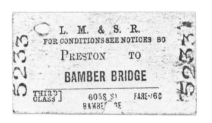

65. Gregson Lane, late 1890's. The Midland Railway had running powers over the LYR from Hellifield to Liverpool. Here a Johnson 4-4-0 heads a Liverpool train approaching Gregson Lane crossing, between Hoghton and Bamber Bridge. *Photo: Author's collection*

Hoghton, c.1900. The station was built about this time, and is seen here when new. *Photo: Author's collection*

Hoghton, January 1953. The signal box was renewed in the early 1900s with a standard LYR design and typical level crossing gates. Both have now gone. *Photo: Author*

8. Lostock Hall Junction, c.1960. A view looking west, with ex-WD 2-10-0 No 0552 taking two wagons and a brake van off the line from Farington Junction. The line straight ahead is to Lostock Hall station, and the loco shed coaling tower can be seen in the distance. *Photo: J. Yates*

69. Lostock Hall, March 1968. A train of coal empties is taken through Lostock Hall by class 8F 2-8-0 No 48062. The engine shed yard is on the left.

Photo: John M. Hammond

70. Lostock Hall, 4th May 1957. Moving on with the 1.12pm Preston to Liverpool train is Stanier Class 5 4-6-0 No 44731. This six coach train stopped at all stations between Preston and Ormskirk before running express to Liverpool Exchange. The corridor coach behind the engine was from Blackpool Central, departing at 12.10pm.

Photo: T. Lewis

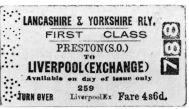

71. Moss Lane Junction. View looking towards Liverpool in LYR days. The right hand line leads in from Farington Curve Junction and Preston.

Photo: Real Photographs

72. Midge Hall, June 1965. The main building is built against the goods shed, hence the need for a tall chimney. Trains from Liverpool to Preston and East Lancashire were usually divided here, even after the station closed in 1961.

Photo: Author

73. Midge Hall, c.1960. A former Lancashire & Yorkshire 0-6-0 engine No 52161 takes a freight train through the station towards Preston. *Photo: J. Yates*

THE RAILWAY STATION, PRESTON.

74. Preston, c.1880. An artist's impression of the Fishergate entrance to the new station, prepared for the 1882 Guild album. The scene is not greatly changed today.

Photo: Author's collection

5: Preston Station

We have seen in the preceding chapters how Preston's railways grew piecemeal from small, local companies that by progressive amalgamations became parts of two large systems. This multiplicity of individual railways in the 1840s resulted in Preston at that time having no less than five stations; the North Union's on the south side of Fishergate, the Bolton & Preston's Maxwell House station to the north, the Lancaster & Preston Junction Railway's terminus at Dock Street close by — which seems to have been little more than a place where passengers joined and left trains, possibly even without a proper platform — the Preston & Wyre's Maudlands station and the Preston & Longridge terminus in Deepdale Street. Some of the Preston & Wyre trains ran into the Fishergate station, which was just as well for passengers bound for more distant parts, as it was over half a mile walk from Maudlands. The Preston & Longridge station, of course, was right on the edge of the town, almost out in the country, over a mile from the main station and completely unconnected by rail. By 1844, however, all except the Longridge company were using the North Union station and four years later the Board of Trade's inspectors were already commenting on its inadequacy, a state of affairs that was to grow much worse and see no real remedy until 1879.

The original 1838 station comprised a 40 ft wide train shed and two platforms. The main entrance building was on the west side of the line, in Italian style which at its opening was described by the *Preston Chronicle* as 'a distinguished ornament to Preston'. The ornament very quickly became tarnished. Although by 1847 two additional sheds had been added to give space for six tracks and four platforms, and the building had been extended, it was done only by dint of making the platforms extremely narrow, and the double track tunnel under Fishergate was a severe bottleneck. When one considers that most trains terminated at Preston, that on the few through trains there was often considerable re-marshalling of carriages, and in any case all trains changed engines, not to mention passengers changing for the Fleetwood, Liverpool, Blackburn and Bolton lines, the chaos can well be imagined. It was compounded by the minimal, often non-existent co-operation between the various companies' staffs. Indeed, after the East Lancashire Railway started using the station in 1846 the North Union deliberately adopted an obstructive policy of preventing proper connections, to the extent that *Bradshaw* in 1851 advised passengers travelling from the north to destinations on the East Lancashire's system not to book tickets beyond Preston, but to enquire for the separate East Lancashire booking office when they got there. The opening of the East Lancashire's 'Extension' line from Lostock Hall and Bamber Bridge eased the cramped conditions slightly when a new

platform was built curving in on the west side, with its own entrance and ticket office in Butler Street.

North of Fishergate tunnel the track layout added to the complications. Until at least 1847 a branch of the canal tramroad crossed the main line by an inadequately protected level crossing to gain access from the canal basin to a coal yard in Pitt Street. Further on there was a second one by which the Preston & Wyre Railway reached its Maudlands station. Although shortly afterwards the tramroad crossing was removed, another was created at Maudlands when the new Longridge line extension crossed the main line in order to reach the Preston & Wyre line. Despite being manned by crossing keepers in charge of primitive signals, the two crossings were a continual source of danger and caused a number of accidents, two of them serious. One, in 1840, was the result of an empty Preston & Wyre passenger train running broadside into a Preston & Lancaster ballast train, killing a man. The other was on a Sunday in 1845 when a Fleetwood excursion composed of goods wagons crammed with passengers, on leaving Maudlands station was cut in half by a train from Lancaster travelling at about 30mph. Surprisingly no one was killed. Both crossings lasted until 1885-86.

The station, meanwhile, continued to gain in decrepitude and disrepute as traffic increased. Preston was notorious for causing delays, accentuated by the meal stop allowed on all north-south expresses before the introduction of dining cars, when passengers made a dash for the refreshment room where they jostled with one another to buy a hot meal and, worse, try to consume it in twenty minutes. The low, narrow platforms were dangerous, and before a footbridge was built in 1857 passengers had to step across the rails to get from one to another. When trains were due the station staff had to escort them across in groups. The *Preston Chronicle* reported that in the 1862 Preston Guild week about half a million passengers used the station, and on one evening 'all the leading entrances to the station, all the platforms within and all the passages without, were absolutely choked up with men and women and children, and hundreds of them could not get away until midnight.' In 1866 part of the roof fell in, the year in which the *Preston Guardian* called the confusion 'without parallel in any other station in the kingdom.' Deputations from the corporation to the railway companies and to the Board of Trade had no effect, and Preston's reputation even spread to the London press.

The trouble stemmed directly from the original rivalry between the North Union and the East Lancashire companies which, despite joint ownership of the station from 1846, was perpetuated by their successors the London & North Western and the Lancashire & Yorkshire, who were never able to agree on the sharing of costs. Indeed, in 1852 no less a person than I K Brunel was called upon to adjudicate on which parts of the station belonged to whom, and where the boundaries between East Lancashire and North Union property lay, so confused had the situation become. At length, in 1873 they finally agreed that improvements could be put off no longer and a start was made on large scale enlargement. The first job was to get rid of Fishergate tunnel and widen the northern approaches. A bridge replaced the tunnel, spanning eight tracks, and in 1879 a spacious new island platform was opened beneath a lofty iron and glass roof. Further extensions were made in 1880, 1903 and 1913, when the station reached its largest extent with five island platforms which, together with bays, provided a total of fifteen platform faces. These included the old East Lancashire platform curving out towards Vicars Bridge, which was replaced by two through platform faces and two bays.

At last the station could deal efficiently with the traffic, although Preston Guild still stretched even the new facilities, and the old practice of using the goods stations when traffic was particularly heavy had to be revived for Guild week, including the old Longridge terminus in Deepdale Street. The size of the problem is indicated by the figures for the 1922 Guild, when over 550,000 return tickets were issued to Preston (including nearly a quarter of a million on the Saturday), close on 49,000 were sold at the station booking offices, and 504 special trains were run. Railway officials doubtless were thankful that the Guild was held only every twenty years.

In 1879 a new main entrance from Fishergate bridge was opened by the joint companies, and a year later a new entrance and booking office solely for the LYR in Butler Street, to be replaced by a third on that side of the station during the 1913 extensions. These separate entrances marked the curiously divided management of the station, under which the three main island platforms were jointly owned and operated by a joint stationmaster and staff, while the East Lancashire platforms were the property of the Lancashire & Yorkshire alone, which had its own staff and stationmaster, an anachronism that lasted until both railways amalgamated in 1921.

The completion of the series of curves and junctions in the Lostock Hall area in 1908 also played a part in the station improvements. As well as allowing LYR Blackpool trains to use the west side of the station without obstructing the main line, the arrangement was equally valuable in avoiding the need to reverse Blackpool trains to and from the north, with attendant engine changes. This routing provided the novelty of seeing a train pass southward through the station on the eastern side and about twenty minutes later return in the opposite direction on the west side, often without stopping, having 'boxed the compass' via Preston Junction, Lostock Hall and Farington Curve Junction, or vice versa, doubtless thoroughly confusing the passengers in the process.

Simplification of the track layout and rationalisation of services in 1971-72 in connection with the West Coast Main Line electrification reduced the station in size. Trains on the Blackburn and Ormskirk lines were concentrated on the route via Farington Curve Junction, enabling the East Lancashire platforms and the 'Extension' line to be closed. Earlier the westernmost island platform, dating from 1903, had lost its overall roof and was now confined to parcels traffic. The old LYR Butler Street entrance was closed but lingered on until 1985, disused, until it, too, disappeared to make way for a new main entrance on which at the time of writing work is still progressing. It is to be hoped that the resultant labyrinthine tour to reach platforms 1 and 2 via the ticket office will also receive attention before long.

For many years the Park Hotel was one of the north west's premier hotels. An imposing building with a fine view overlooking Avenham and Miller Parks and the river, it was designed for the joint railways by Arnold Mitchell, an Oldham architect, and opened in 1882. A private covered way and footbridge connected it directly to the platforms at the south end of the station. In 1950 Lancashire County Council bought it for use as offices, and the footbridge was demolished.

75. **Preston, c.1915.** Former Platform 5 (now No 3) looking south.

Photo: V. R. Anderson collection

76. Preston, March 1952. The LY[...]
separate entrance in Butler Street, built [...]
1913 and demolished in 1985.

Photo: Auth[...]

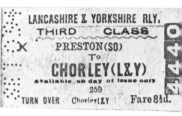

No.77. Preston. July 1955. Platforms [...]
and 7 (now 4 and 5), looking sou[th]
showing the central crossovers. Th[e]
colour light signal on platform 7 for th[e]
crossovers and access to the E. L. line
is believed to have been in operatio[n]
during the war.

Photo: V.R. Anderson collectio[n]

No.78. Preston. 1948. A mixture [of]
LNWR lower quadrant and LMS upp[er]
quadrant signals on the gantry at th[e]
south end of Platform 5. The signal bo[x]
to the right of and framed by the structur[e]
is No.1A. *Photo: LGRP*

79. Preston, 1961. Rebuilt 'Royal Scot' No 46155 *The Lancer* starts away from platform 4 with a Blackpool train.
Photo: B. C. Lane

80. Preston, Early 1900's. A gleaming LYR 2-4-2 tank No 705 stands in the shadow of the footbridge on the centre road between the north ends of Platforms 2 and 3. *Photo: Real Photographs Co*

81. Preston, April 1939. 'Royal Scot' loco No 6108 *Seaforth Highlander* sets out under Fishergate bridge with a north-bound express. *Photo: E. R. Morten*

82. Preston. March 1968. Class 5 4-6-0 No.**44967** waits to depart with a Barrow train at the north end of platform 8 (now 6).   *John M. Hammond*

83. Preston, c.1959. A grimy 0-8-0 No 49382 takes a heavy freight southwards through the west side of the station beneath the partly dismantled footbridge to the former Park Hotel.

Photo: J. Yates

84. Preston, March 1952. The now demolished East Lancashire Platforms 12 and 13, with a Liverpool train standing in bay Platform 11. *Photo: Author*

85. Preston, c.1921. A view from Vicars bridge as an LYR 2-4-2 tank shunts a passenger train on the East Lancashire line overlooking Avenham Park, with the Ribble beyond. *Photo: Author's collection*

86. Preston, March 1964. Another view from Vicars Bridge, looking the other way into the station. The East Lancashire platforms are on the right. *Photo: Martin Welch*

ACCIDENT
TO SCOTCH EXPRESS
PRESTON. JULY. 13TH 1896. (COPYRIGHT)

87. (Above) Preston, 1896. On 13 July the down Scotch sleeping car express, double headed by LNWR 2-4-0 engines Nos 275 *Vulcan* and 2159 *Shark*, came to grief when taking the sharp curve north of the station at 40mph instead of the prescribed 10mph. Only the locomotives and one of the seven coaches remained upright. Wreckage was scattered over a wide area, as this picture taken from the old Canal Foundry in what is now Barracks Street shows, yet incredibly only one person was killed.

Photo: courtesy Harris Museum

88. (Left) Preston, Park Hotel. Many 19th century railways published picture postcards. Although this one rightly bears the imprint of the LNWR and LYR, for the hotel was jointly owned, the Britannia emblem indicated that it was the LNWR that actually published it. *Photo: Author's collection*

89. (Below) Preston, c.1957. This stirring sight south of Preston shows Stanier "Princess Coronation" Class 7P 4-6-2 No 46228 *Duchess of Rutland* approaching Skew Bridge with an up relief train of 16 coaches bound for Euston. Well known examples of the Preston skyline are prominent to the rear of the train, Park Hotel being the most readily identifiable. *Photo: T. Lewis*

90. Preston, 1947-48. An aerial view of Preston town centre showing the station, goods yards and, lower left, the Park Hotel overlooking the river. The North Union and East Lancashire railway bridges can be seen and, far right, the Old Tram bridge.

Photo: Airviews (Manchester) Ltd

91. Whitehouse South Junction, 4th July 1957. Agecroft based Class 5 4-6-0 No 45338 pulls away from Preston with a Brindle Heath-bound fitted freight. The West Lancashire line curves away to the left of the signal box to form a triangle with the direct curve from Preston station, thereby allowing through running of trains from both directions.

Photo: T. Lewis

6: The West Lancashire Railway

At the beginning of the 1882 Preston Guild a new railway was opened from Southport. The new station at the bottom of Fishergate Hill was hastily made ready for excursionists, but formal opening of the West Lancashire Railway for regular passenger services did not take place until a week later. Promoted by Southport interests who sought to break the monopoly of the Lancashire & Yorkshire Railway and provide a shorter route between the two towns than via Burscough, the line was under-capitalised and, running through thinly populated rural districts, was unlikely to produce much revenue. Consequently its finances at best were shaky and, built in sections as money allowed, not surprisingly it took all of eleven years to complete 15¾ miles of railway.

Yet, full of confidence, the company tried to do things in style, from the grand opening celebrations to its substantial, brick-built stations and elaborate, needlessly large termini. The Preston station was a smaller edition of the terminus in Derby Road at Southport, of stone in a Gothic style designed by Charles H Driver, a Westminster architect known for his railway work. In 1883 a triangular junction was opened at Preston leading to a short branch on to the Lancashire & Yorkshire's East Lancashire line at Whitehouse Junction, enabling the smaller company to run through trains from Southport to Blackburn.

This rose-tinted outlook characterised most of the West Lancashire's policy. From the outset the directors realised that as a self-contained line the company could not succeed, and they optimistically tried to portray their railway as a strategic link in larger schemes. Southport was not the only place that disliked the LYR's monopoly. Preston, Blackpool and other towns in the Fylde were equally concerned to get better railway rates and services by introducing competition. Back in 1873, with construction hardly begun, one of the West Lancashire's leading promoters had unsuccessfully suggested to the Manchester Sheffield & Lincolnshire Railway that it might lease the West Lancashire when it was finished. It was known that the MSLR, an aggressively expansionist company, was actively seeking to gain a share

of the lucrative Blackpool traffic by promoting a separate line from Manchester with the full support of the local authorities. But the MSLR was not prepared to commit itself without seeing some tangible results.

Then in 1882, when at last the line was ready, the West Lancashire directors proposed to build their own line to Blackpool from Hesketh Bank, crossing the Ribble by a long and expensive bridge to Freckleton, but were deterred by opposition from Preston Corporation which was about to acquire and improve the river navigation. So the directors once more approached the MSLR, this time with greater success. That company was already backing an independent line from Manchester to Wigan — completed in 1884 — as the first part of its drive for Blackpool, and partly as a result of the West Lancashire's overtures obtained parliamentary powers in 1883 to extend the Wigan line to join the West Lancashire at Longton. At the same time Blackpool, Preston and other Fylde local authorities sent a delegation that included Preston's mayor and town clerk to press their case on the MSLR which, now armed with the local support it wanted, proceeded to promote a satellite company called the Blackpool Railway. The following year it obtained an Act for a line from the West Lancashire at Preston to Blackpool, thereby creating the final link in the chain, albeit only a paper one. Simultaneously the West Lancashire itself obtained a further Act, for a short extension to Preston Dock that would form the commencement of the new line.

Meanwhile, the West Lancashire was fast losing money. Revenue was insufficient to cover operating expenses, so in 1885 it again tried to persuade the MSLR to work its trains. The latter, fully aware of the situation, for the moment declined, wisely from its point of view, as in 1886 the West Lancashire succumbed to insolvency and an official receiver was appointed; the MSLR, despite its big ideas, had refused to come to the rescue. Indeed, it was starting to lose interest. Much more ambitious proposals were now germinating for a new line to London, in which it eventually succeeded, although at severe financial cost.

Consequently, despite periodic urgings from Blackpool and Preston corporations, the Blackpool Railway never became reality, although the project was not legally abandoned until 1896. In a final desperate fling the West Lancashire became involved in one of the even less realistic railway schemes that were promoted towards the end of the century, a madcap project aimed at making a new route between north west and north east England. It was in a way a revival of the schemes promoted forty years earlier that involved the Preston & Longridge line. This one was grandly called the North West Central Railway, and proposed to build a line that would require very heavy engineering works across hilly country to connect Bradford, Halifax and Keighley direct with Preston and Liverpool, using the West Lancashire between Penwortham and Southport. It even got an Act in 1890 and another, abandoning the idea, in 1893.

In 1894 the West Lancashire was empowered to reconstruct its finances, a year later actually started making a profit, and in 1897 was absorbed by the company that 26 years earlier it had set out to challenge, the Lancashire & Yorkshire. During that time it had obtained fifteen Acts of Parliament, the legal costs of which alone must have caused a severe drain on its finances. It was a classic example of a local business group forming a small railway company in an attempt to

break the dominance of an established monopoly; full of enthusiasm, pinning their faith in influencing national railway politics but unable to avoid becoming a pawn in a game they were powerless to control, they ended up bankrupt and finally were taken over by the very organisation they had tried to defy.

The new owner immediately set about restoring the sadly deteriorated permanent way and arranging to run trains into its own stations at each end of the line. At Preston this meant building a new west-to-north curve at Whitehouse Junction, completed in 1900 when the Fishergate Hill station was closed to passengers, making the curve between Ribble Junction and Middleforth Junction redundant. It was taken out of use at the same time, but Fishergate Hill remained as a goods station and even saw passenger trains again during Preston Guild weeks.

The Preston end of the West Lancashire almost became important again in 1914 when the LNWR and LYR drew up plans for an avoiding line from Fishergate Hill across the dock estate to the Blackpool line at Lea, to by-pass Preston station at busy periods, but World War 1 prevented any further action. In 1964 the whole of the West Lancashire, including Fishergate Hill goods station, was closed as part of the Beeching cuts after 82 years of life.

92. Whitehouse South Junction, c.1961. A view looking towards Preston, with the West Lancashire connecting line swinging away to the left. The train is an Eastern Region 'foreigner', bound for Yorkshire and hauled by ex-LNER B1 class locomotive No 61145. *Photo: B. Reynolds*

93. Fishergate Hill, 1937. The former West Lancashire terminus, now demolished, was for many years let to a firm of provender merchants as offices. The West Lancashire title was changed to Fishergate Hill in the early years of the century.
Photo: LGRP/David & Charles

94. Fishergate Hill, 1930's. After closure to passengers, the overall roof was retained to form a covered goods depot. Low level cattle sidings can be seen to the left.
Photo: D. Thompson

95. Fishergate Hill, 1930's. A closer view of the former passenger station. The platform occupied the central space.
Photo: D. Thompson

96. West Lancashire Bridge, 1880's. A view looking across the West Lancashire bridge towards Fishergate Hill station, with the old Penwortham Bridge on the left.
Photo: Harris Museum

97. West Lancashire bridge, c.1900. A later view of the bridge showing its plate girder construction. Although it was demolished following closure, the piers remain.

98. Penwortham Cop Lane, June 1954. The first station out of Preston was Penwortham Cop Lane, a halt built by the LYR in 1911 and simply called Cop Lane until 1940, seen here looking towards Southport. *Photo: R. A. Cook*

99. New Longton and Hutton, June 1954. This station was also built by the Lancashire and Yorkshire Railway and opened in 1889 under the name of Howick. It changed to Hutton & Howick in 1897 before taking its final name in 1924. This view is towards Preston. Right up until closure the station enjoyed a fairly comprehensive service with upwards of thirty trains calling to give either a nine minute journey into Preston or thirty minutes to Southport. Sundays gave the station six trains in each direction. *Photo: R. A. Cook*

100. Longton Bridge, 1930's. The first of the original West Lancashire stations after leaving Preston, and until 1892, plain *Longton*. It was built in the company's typical red brick style and is seen here looking towards Preston.
Photo: D. Thompson

101. **Preston Dock.** Two of the dock 0-6-0 saddle tank engines stand outside the shed: *Edinburgh*, a Hawthorn Leslie of 1893 and the first to be bought, and *Queen*, a Peckett built in 1906. Both are fitted with spark arresters for working in the timber yards.   *Photo: Courtesy J. M. Dakres*

7: The Dock Railway

The line down to Preston Dock was built by the North Union Railway under an Act of 1845. The Victoria Quay, with its large bonded warehouse that until 1983 was such a landmark at the bottom of Marsh Lane with its large painted advertisement for Dr Jim's Rum, was completed in 1843, and it was to serve the new quay that the railway was opened in 1846. Under the Act it was constituted as a separate company known as the Ribble Branch Railway. Half of the board of directors were appointed by the railway company and its successors the LNWR and LYR, and half by the Ribble Navigation Company, the costs and expenses being shared equally by each party.

The branch descended from the main line at the south end of Preston station on a steep gradient, part of which was 1 in 29. The sharply curved single line passed through a 145yd tunnel at the foot of Fishergate Hill, beyond which there was an acute-angled level crossing over Strand Road, after which it became solely Navigation Company property. Later, sidings were built from the dock lines into an adjacent wagon works which later became the West Works of Dick, Kerr & Co, builders of electric tramcars. Another siding crossed back over West Strand into the East Works. Both became part of the English Electric Company, now GEC. There were also sidings into Stevensons' engineering works and Page & Taylor's sawmills in Watery Lane, the latter also reached by a level crossing.

From 1870 successive agreements were made with the joint railway companies to maintain and operate the branch themselves on a toll basis, part of which went to the Navigation Company. Then in 1882 the borough corporation acquired the navigation expressly to develop Preston as a major port. Over the next seven years the river channel was diverted and a 40 acre dock constructed, opened in 1892 and at that time the largest in the country. The Albert Edward Dock had 1½ miles of quays and, ultimately, some 28 miles of railway track.

Between the wars and until the 1960s the dock was busy, with considerable expansion taking place in the 1920s and during the second world war, but in the 1970s the general decline of Britain's west coast ports was accentuated at Preston by the tidal approach, and after heavy financial losses the dock closed in 1979. The railway was still needed to serve industrial sites on the dock estate, however, and in connection with the corporation's redevelopment scheme to create a marina, leisure complex, housing and a light industrial estate, the railway recently was completely re-routed on a new alignment between the south side of the dock and the river. This has entailed construction of a road and rail swing bridge across the dock entrance to reach the industrial area. Further west a new engine shed has been built, carefully designed to blend with the projected development, for which in 1986 it won a Brick Development Association award. The new railway has some five miles of track, including sidings.

Preston Corporation over the years had a fleet of eight steam locomotives, all 0-6-0 saddle tanks except one, a fireless locomotive which was charged with steam at a dockside boiler house and used in the petrol storage yards established from 1915 onwards. There was also a diesel locomotive purchased in 1935. In 1968 it was decided to dispense with the entire fleet and purchase three Rolls-Royce Sentinel 4-wheel diesel-hydraulic locomotives, which by that time were adequate for the traffic. All the steam engines were scrapped, except *Princess,* a 1942 Bagnall which went to the preserved Lakeside & Haverthwaite Railway in Cumbria. It was also a nice touch to use the nameplates from three of the old steam engines on the new diesels: *Energy, Enterprise* and *Progress.* A fourth diesel, a 4-wheel Planet locomotive, belongs to Lancashire Tar Distilleries and is used for shunting their yard at the dock.

The dock engines take over from British Rail at the exchange sidings just inside the dock gates at Strand Road crossing. Before electrification and re-signalling of the main line, the Ribble Branch was operated by electric train staff between Preston No 1A signal box and a small cabin at Strand Road. Over the 40-50 years up to the end of steam working the usual engines employed on the branch were LNWR 0-8-0s. Up trains were limited to about 30 loaded wagons or 50 coal empties, requiring engines at the front and the rear, while up to 70 wagons were allowed on descending trains. The line rises out of a narrow brick-lined cutting to the west of the south end of Preston station, until 197? straddled by No 2A signal box on a gantry. From the platforms it was an impressive sight to see one of these engines bursting, as it were, from the bowels of the earth, enveloping the box in smoke and steam, to be followed a few minutes later by a second one banking at the rear.

102. (Above-left) Preston Dock, c.1938.
The 1937 Barclay 0-6-0 fireless locomotive *Duke*, with a train of petrol tankers.
Photo: J. M. Dakres

105. (Above) Preston Dock, 1930's. The Barclay 0-6-0 saddle tank *Prince* (1923) with a rake of wagons on the south side of the dock. *Photo: Courtesy J. M. Dakres*

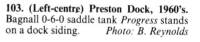

103. (Left-centre) Preston Dock, 1960's.
Bagnall 0-6-0 saddle tank *Progress* stands on a dock siding. *Photo: B. Reynolds*

104. (Left) Preston Dock, 1968. Farewell to steam – the last working of Bagnall 0-6-0 saddle tank *Princess* (1942). Strand Road is on the other side of the fence.
Photo: Courtesy Keith Fletcher

106. Preston Dock, c.1937. The exchange sidings with the shape of things to come in the form of Armstrong Whitworth 0-6-0 Diesel Electric shunting engine. Compare this view with the motive power on display in the picture below.

Photo: Harris Museum

107. Preston Dock, pre 1923. With a full head of steam, a LNWR 0-8-0 prepares to take a full load from the exchange sidings up the branch to Preston station. Preston shed kept three of these engines for this duty, and in 1952 there were 12 trips a day to and from the dock, including coal for the conveyor to the power station across the river. *Photo: Harris Museum*

108. Ribble Branch, 1952. Former LNWR 0-8-0 No 49382 blasts its way up the Ribble Branch from Fishergate Hill tunnel, alongside the back gardens of North Cliff Street.

Photo: R. B. Holden

109. Preston, c.1962. No 2A signal box was perched over the narrow brick walled cutting through which the Ribble Branch emerges into the station precincts. Indeed, few will forget the sight and sounds of the LNWR 0-8-0s making their way up from the docks past Strand Road. The signal box had a 40 lever frame with 10 spare and dated from 1887. Christian Road goods warehouses are to the left of the picture, a site later to be occupied by the Post Office's centralized sorting office.

Photo: G. H. Platt

110. Preston, c.1960. The northern approaches to Preston passed beneath this large signal gantry on a falling gradient from Maudland viaduct. To the left of No 4 signal box is the engine pulling the train from which the photograph is taken, Fowler "Patriot" 5XP 4-6-0 No 45513, an un-rebuilt and un-named member of the class. The engine alongside is "Jubilee" class 4-6-0 No 45697 *Achilles*. The lower quadrant signals of the LNWR have been replaced by upper quadrant arms. *Photo: B. C. Lane*

8: Operating the Railway

Many facets of railway operating are now far removed from the methods of only twenty years ago, none perhaps more so than signalling, locomotive servicing and the handling of freight.

It is not until they have gone that one realises the prominence that mechanical signalling equipment had in the railway scene. The disappearance of arrays of semaphore signals and numerous signal boxes, accompanied by simplified track layouts, has removed something of the character of many a large station, leaving a bare look that unwinking electric colour light signals do little to replace. Preston is a good example. Before modernisation the approaches were guarded by large gantries of signals, until the 1950s comprising mostly former LNWR lower quadrant arms that afterwards were gradually replaced by standard BR upper quadrant types. Half way along the main platforms, beneath the overall roof, the scene was dominated by large LNWR bracket signals, right up to the end of the mechanical era. On the East Lancashire side some LYR signals remained until the 1960s, rather neater in style than the LNWR types.

The station area had seven signal boxes, numbered 1-5 from the southern end to Maudlands Junction where the Blackpool and Lancaster lines diverged, with the addition of No 1A controlling Christian Road goods yard entrance and the Ribble Branch, and No 2A the through goods line that passed outside the station on the west. Nos 2 and 3 were under the station roof itself, the former controlling the main line scissors crossings in the middle of the station and the latter access to the East Lancashire line. An eighth box, named East Lancashire Goods, was an LYR structure close to the East Lancashire bridge over the Ribble, controlling trains entering and leaving that side of the station and Butler Street goods yard. On the main line just south of the station there was Ribble Siding box, where marshalling of freight trains to and from Christian Road goods yard and the dock branch took

place. On the Blackpool line just beyond the junction stood Maudland Viaduct box, and a short distance along the Longridge branch there was Maudland Curve box dealing with traffic for Maudlands goods station. These two boxes perpetuated the apparent uncertainty over the final 's' which seems to have existed from the earliest days. Additionally to all these signal boxes there were ten more further out, but still within the immediate Preston area, and nine on the LYR lines around Lostock Hall and Bamber Bridge, all in all employing about a hundred signalmen when they were open around the clock. Now the whole area and many miles of radiating lines are operated from a single power box north of the station, operated by six men.

Originally each railway entering Preston had its own engine shed. The North Union's was on the east side of the station in Butler Street where it also had repair shops, and the Preston & Wyre kept their engines at Maudlands. The Lancaster & Preston company's shed was on the west side of Maudlands Junction and in 1850 had eight roads and a turntable. It was also used by the Lancaster & Carlisle Railway, who built a new one there in 1857, and the site was later used by the LNWR. At the end of the 1930s the shed was reduced in size to make space for mechanical coaling and ash plant. In 1960 a fire destroyed most of the roof, and as closure was imminent it was not repaired. The following year the engines were transferred to Lostock Hall which for the last few years of steam became the sole shed serving Preston. The power signal box now occupies the site.

The Blackburn & Preston Railway had a small shed housing two engines in the fork of the junction at Farington, but it was not used for long. The East Lancashire Railway and its successor the LYR used the LNWR shed north of the station, but also had a 5-road shed in the angle of the junction with the main line on the Butler Street side, with a 50ft turntable and a carriage shed. Then in 1881 the LYR opened a large new eight-road locomotive depot at Lostock Hall which in 1945 had a location of 51 engines. It had a 60ft turntable, and was one of the last steam sheds to remain open on British Railways, closing in 1968.

The little West Lancashire Railway also had a locomotive shed at its Fishergate Hill terminus, with two tracks and a turntable, which was closed after the amalgamation with the LYR.

As one would expect at a large industrial town like Preston, the railway age provided extensive facilities for handling freight which, although it had none of the glamour of fast passenger trains, was the mainstay of the railways. The former North Union goods yard was approached from Charles Street on the west side of the station, but for later extensions it was demolished and a new street made called Christian Road, which gave its name to the enlarged LNWR goods depot. The LYR's was on the opposite side of the station in Butler Street. Both had large warehouses. General freight was also handled at the West Lancashire yard at the bottom of Fishergate Hill, at the old Preston & Wyre yard at Maudlands, and at the original Preston & Longridge terminus in Deepdale Street which also handled coal. There were two extensive coal yards on the east side of the main line north of Fishergate, called Dock Street and Corporation Street, although they

really functioned as one in later years and dated back to the days of the canal tramroad.

Further north the LNWR had an extensive yard called Greenbank Sidings, which it acquired in 1906 from a private company that had operated it on behalf of a number of coal merchants and local firms, including the adjacent Soho Foundry. It was opened about 1881 and during private ownership had two 0-4-0 saddle tank engines for shunting, and a small shed. Further north still, on the north side of Blackpool Road, Oxheys cattle sidings were located next to the market. For many years a special platform on the east side of the line south of the bridge served the market, at which two early morning up trains called twice a week to set down passengers. The service ceased in 1925 but the platform remained until the 1960s. Livestock was also handled at Butler Street, Fishergate Hill and Maudlands.

A large centralised postal sorting office now occupies the site of Christian Road yard, the once numerous sidings reduced to just two for Post Office traffic. Today it is difficult to imagine the volume of goods once carried by rail, and that in 1927, in addition to all these public goods yards, there were as many as 32 private sidings in Preston.

111. (Above) Preston, June 1953. The southern approaches to Preston station were protected by this lofty array of LNWR signals on the North Union bridge. The Park Hotel is on the right.
Photo: British Rail

112. (Left) Preston, June 1953. They were controlled from No 1 signal box, which had 138 working levers and was operated by three men, as seen here. It was second in size only to No 4 box which had 170 levers. The lever frame, instruments and fittings form a typical LNWR signal box interior.
Photo: British Rail

113. Preston, March 1952. LYR signals were smaller, with spiked finials. Platforms 11 and 12 signals were always dirty from engine smoke. Vicars Bridge and East Lancashire Goods box are in the background. *Photo: Author*

115. Preston, June 1953. The large bracket signals on what is now Platform protecting the central cross-overs which allowed two trains to use the long platforms. Like the pigeon baskets, they are reminders of a different age.
Photo: British R

114. Preston, August 1953. At the north end of the station there was insufficient space for full size signal arms, so special shortened versions were fitted. These were o Platforms 3 and 6.
Photo: T. Lew

116. (Above-left) Preston, June 1954. Signalling on the Preston & Wyre joint line was the responsibility of the LYR. Maudland Viaduct box down home signals were of later pattern, peering over the railings alongside St Marks Road. *Photo: Author*

117. (Above-right) Maudland Curve, 28th August 1964. Maudland Curve signal box was one of the smallest structures and controlled the sidings leading off the Longridge branch alongside Maudland Road. The bridge parapet overlooks the canal running under the railway and the site of Maudland Bridge station was immediately to the right. The signal box was destroyed by fire some eight months later and officially closed from 14th April 1965. A temporary block post was set up in an adjacent platelayers' cabin, movements being controlled by hand signalmen. The damaged structure was taken away on 16th May 1965 and its signalling functions replaced by a ground frame situated alongside. *Photo: G. Coltas*

118. Preston–Ribble Siding, June 1953. This view towards Preston from the south shows the new signal box which replaced the structure in the distance. The redundant box dated from 1902 and was itself a replacement for an earlier unit of 1880. Electrification of the West Coast main line and subsequent commissioning of a new power box rendered this and numerous other boxes redundant on 5th February 1973. *Photo: British Rail*

119. Maudlands Junction, 28th August 1964. Last of the large Preston signal boxes was No 5, a typical LNWR structure with a total of 114 working levers. The line to Carlisle runs straight ahead and to the right of St. Walburge's church. The Longridge branch disappears around the back of the signal box. The line to the left is to Blackpool and Fleetwood. *Photo: G. Coltas*

120. Preston, c.1959. No 3 signal box was partly under the station roof on the east side and controlled a junction with the East Lancashire lines curving to the left. This composite structure, i.e. brick base, wooden upper, dated from 1882 and had a frame of 31 levers of which 15 were for points and the remainder signals. It is interesting to note that an LNWR survey of 1910 gave box and apparatus a life expectancy of seventeen years! The Park Hotel footbridge can be seen beyond the station roof.

Photo: G. H. Platt

121. Preston-East Lancashire Goods box, c.1959. This box originally belonged to the Lancashire & Yorkshire Railway and is of quite different design compared with the ex-LNWR boxes in the station proper. It controlled the approaches to the East Lancashire platforms and Butler Street goods yard. The view is from Vicar Bridge.

Photo: G. H. Platt

122. Preston Shed, 26th April 1949. A quiet moment on shed with Class 5 No 5414 and "Patriot" No 45519 *Lady Godiva* perhaps contemplating whom they actually belong to. The former still bears its LMS smokebox number plate and the latter has received a new BR number whilst retaining the mark of its former owners on the tender. The roof of this former LNWR shed was partially reconstructed in 1936 along with other improvements. *Photo: H. C. Casserley*

123. Preston Shed, 26th April 1949. 2-6-4 tank engine No 2476 stands alongside the turntable beside the depot. Croft Street mill – now demolished – stands in the background. It had a short private siding which served the premises. The semi-circular concrete sections in the foreground remain from wartime air raid shelters, when countless railwaymen and women were forced to take cover from air attack. *Photo: H. C. Casserley*

124. (Below) Preston Shed, c.1961. A full but silent depot stands awaiting its fate shortly after the June fire when roof and some offices were destroyed. "Patriot" No 45507 *Royal Tank Corps* is the only identifiable locomotive amongst the numerous ex-LNWR 0-8-0's. The coaling plant was erected in 1936 by the LMS, along with other improvements. *Photo: G. H. Platt*

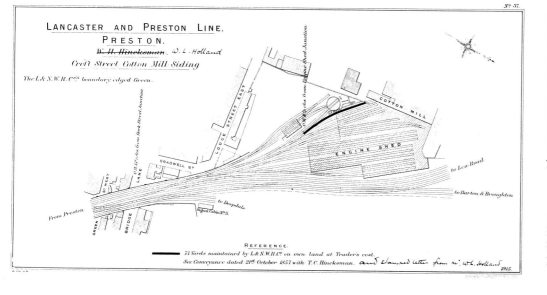

LANCASTER AND PRESTON LINE.
PRESTON.
~~W. H. Hincksman.~~ W. L. Holland
Croft Street Cotton Mill Siding

The L. & N. W. R. Cos boundary edged Green.

COTTON MILL

ENGINE SHED

to Lea Road

to Barton & Broughton

to Deepdale

From Preston

GREEN
BRIDGE

Signal Cabin N°5.

REFERENCE.
~~73 Yards maintained by L. & N. W. R. Cos on own land at Traders cost.~~
See Conveyance dated 21st October 1857 with T. C. Hincksman. and stamped letter from mr Wm L. Holland
1915.

126. (Above) Preston, July 1961. The shape of things to come with diesels standing amidst the burnt out remains of the shed. Rounding the curve from the Fylde line is Class 5 No 44729 with a summer "Saturdays Only" train to Newcastle. Historically, this train had left Blackpool North at 11.35am and passed Preston at 12.5pm. This was one of the trains to be routed regularly southward through Preston, round the Farington and Lostock Hall curves and then, some 14 minutes later, pass through the station a second time in the northbound direction. The journey to Newcastle continued via Lancaster and Carlisle. *Photo: J. M. Hammond*

125. (Inset) Preston Shed, c.1961. Following the fire, the depot briefly became the home of diesel shunting engines, one visitor being No D2862 – later class 02 – an 0-4-0 Diesel Hydraulic locomotive.

Photo: S. Withers

127. Lostock Hall Shed, August 1968.
Three days following closure, the depot has literally become a graveyard for the steam locomotive although in the middle distance a Class 5 defies the inevitable, perhaps for just a few more hours. Lostock Hall continued in use for diesel maintenance and later as an engineering depot.
Photo: F. Elliott

128. Lostock Hall Shed, May 1957.
Former LYR 2-4-2 tank engine takes water inside the shed yard alongside a pair of Stanier Class 4 2-6-4T locomotives.
Photo: Author

129. Lostock Hall. Bank Hall based class 2 4-4-0 No 40684 pulls away from the station with a train from Liverpool Exchange to Preston, as indicated by the signals showing above the bridge parapet.
Photo: J. Yates

130. Preston–Butler Street Goods Depot, 1860's. Viewed from Vicars Bridge, this early photograph shows the East Lancashire Railway engine shed to the left. Beyond, in the middle distance is the LNWR Charles Street goods yard. The fencing to the right of the engine shed forms the back of the ELR platform. The two buildings to the right with arched entrances were the ELR Carriage Shed and Goods Warehouse respectively. The vehicles in front of the former are four-wheel carriages. *Photo: Harris Museum*

131. Preston, February 1973. This lofty warehouse, still with the LYR's name on the roof, was familiar to motorists using the station after the goods yard closed and was partly converted into a car park. It has since been demolished to make way for the Asda store car park. *Photo: Author*

132. Preston–Ribble Sidings, c.1938. Aspinall-designed 0-6-0 goods engine No 12619 accelerates up the grade past Ribble Sidings with a southbound freight. Although approaching its thirtieth birthday this locomotive still had some fifteen years of life left in it before being withdrawn in 1953. Entering service in August 1909 as Lancashire and Yorkshire Railway No 887, its appearance was changed somewhat with the substitution of a Belpaire boiler in 1922. *Photo: Eric Treacy*

133. Preston–Greenbank Sidings, c.1956. Pulling out of Preston heading north is Lancaster-based LMS "Compound" 4-4-0 No 41065 with a summer "Saturdays Only" working to Morecambe Euston Road, and containing through carriages from Manchester Victoria. "Steam Mill", to the right of the picture, stands between the Lancaster Canal and Fylde Road. Greenbank Sidings, which many years ago served a number of industrial premises, closed in 1966, although the signal box, situated at the southern end of the quadrupled section to Barton and Broughton, lingered on until 1969. *Photo: R. B. Holden*

134. Greenbank Sidings, c.1952. The last remaining member of the class, No 47862, is seen in Greenbank Yard. These ex LNWR 0-4-2 saddle tank engines, were designed with a short wheelbase and were ideal for shunting on the sharp curves. It was allocated to Preston shed.
Photo: C. Garstang

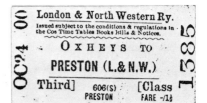

135. (Below) Oxheys, July 1937. The northbound 'Coronation Scot' headed by 4-6-2 No 6224 *Princess Alexandra* passes the special cattle market platform that up to 1925 was used for the twice weekly market. Eldon Street bridge is in the background. *Photo: E. R. Morten*

No.136. Preston. 11th June 1953. Much has been said of Preston's "celebrated" signal boxes. The London and North Western Railway certainly opted for things on a grand scale when enlarging Preston station around the turn of the century. No.4 box was situated immediately to the north of Fishergate bridge, adjacent to the Down Fast (Carlisle) line. Built in 1902, it was a composite (brick base, timber upper) structure 12 feet in width and 104 feet in length, although the latter was the result of a short extension (4 feet) carried out some seven years later. Its extensive frame constituted 72 levers which operated points and another 101 for signal movements. Life expectancy in 1910 was no more than 37 years, so this view shows the box in the sixth year of borrowed time!

British Rail.

No.137. Preston. 23rd July 1952. This view from the east end of Fishergate bridge shows No.4. signal box to the left. There are shiny rails all around, none more than those serving Dock Street Coal Yard to the left.

British Rail.

Station Working for the 1922 Guild.

The London & North Western Railway was at the receiving end of the influx of additional traffic for the Preston Guild Week and took elaborate precautions to ensure that their involvement passed off as smoothly as possible. Traffic working arrangements for 1922, which occurred from 6th to 9th September, and coincided with the Royal Lancashire Agricultural Show on those days, extended the skills and ingenuity of all the railways different departments to the full. It must be borne in mind that amalgamation with the Lancashire & Yorkshire Railway had come into effect from 1st January of the same year. The LNWR Northern Division was referred to as Division "A", whilst the former L&Y was called Division "B", although little integration had taken place between the two companies by this time. In certain instances, however, there was a combining of information into single publications, as in this specific instance.

To ensure that everyone involved with the programme of events was familiar with the routine, a special publication was issued by Ashton Davies, the General Superintendent of the Northern Division Office in Manchester, publication No.162, which extended to 144 sides, outlining the procedures to be adopted for every type of traffic. The booklet outlined the temporary accommodation provided for the use of the passenger department, the general arrangements for passenger and goods traffic, special arrangements for goods trains including the re-routing of some traffic over the Midland Company's line via Ingleton and Hellifield; special requirements for the Royal Agricultural Show and alterations to the hours of working at signal boxes and for traffic department staff.

Four additional sets of sidings were required for the Passenger Department. Freight traffic normally dealt with at Preston (E.L.) Goods Yard was transferred to the Northern Union yard at Christian Road, Farington Coal Sidings (Slow Line Sidings) were worked through to Bamfurlong, P.& W. Line, Farington (Balloon Sidings) Fast Line Sidings, Ribble Sidings traffic was concentrated at Springs Branch Preston Line, Longridge, Farington (Fast Line Sidings), Lostock Hall and Bamber Bridge, and for Lostock Hall Carriage Sidings, from Division "B" were worked by through trains after being concentrated at Rose Grove, Church (Exchange Sidings), Blackburn (Taylor Street) and Bamber Bridge.

In the General Notes - Goods Train Traffic section, disposal and working of specific trains and at specific points was outlined, with Mr Range of the General Superintendent's Department installed at Preston for the week, and who accepted responsibility for all Goods Train Arrangements. Modification and alteration to Division 'A' traffic for specific LNWR section trains was outlined in detail. In some instances this involved re-timing specific trains, in other cases the traffic was re-routed, and some local pick-up freight trains were cancelled on specific days. Most of the through freight workings between Birmingham, Camden, Crewe and Carlisle were re-routed via Ingleton and Hellifield. Most Friday night and Saturday through trains were terminated short of their destination on either side of Preston, those containing perishable traffic which could not be held up being limited in their loading and routed away from the station wherever possible.

Most trip and shunting engine workings were suspended between 10.00pm on Sunday September 3rd, until midnight on Saturday September 9th. There were some exceptions, and where freight traffic was diverted to other yards, extra locomotive and crews were provided to cover the additional work. The section states that power requirements on the weekends prior to and following the Guild Week were arranged locally by Preston Control in accordance with requirements. These included clearing Farington and Ribble Sidings of standing freight stock on Sunday 3rd September, to make room for special traffic passenger stock.

Goods Train Arrangements for Division "B", from former L&Y destinations were altered significantly, with many trains withdrawn, and the remainder retimed and re-routed to avoid the platform lines through the station. In the section marked 'Classification of Goods Trains', those trains that were required to run were modified to take up traffic from cancelled trains.

There was a similar disruption to engine, enginemen and guards workings, and the Division "B" alterations run to seven pages.

Alterations to passenger trains was more profound. Transfer of vehicles at the station was suspended unless special dispensation was given, and some through carriage workings that took place at the station were altered. For example, the 9.30am Southport to Glasgow through coach was cancelled, although the balancing 10.10am Glasgow to Southport working ran. The coach was worked back to Manchester Victoria the same evening on the 7.00pm working, and travelled north with the 9.40am Manchester (Victoria) to Glasgow the next morning. The same fate befell the 12.10pm Blackpool (C) to Glasgow. The 7.50am Blackpool (C) to Euston was similarly axed, as was the 8.30am Windermere to Liverpool Exchange and the 5.08pm return working back to Windermere.

It was decreed that wherever possible, engines would not take water at Preston, and wherever possible, no engine changes were made at the station. There was no provision allowed to turn engines at Preston (E.L.) between 6.30am and midnight.

It was decreed that all trains, both ordinary and special, stopping at Preston after 3.00pm had to carry a label board in front of the engine showing the destination of the train. Trains departing from Preston at night had to have destination labels applied to the quarter-lights of the carriages, denoting the stops made.

All special trains were allocated a running number which it carried on each day run. Some trains did not run every day of the week, and this point was made also.

Trains off the East Lancashire line arrived at and departed from The E.L. Goods Yard, with passenger leaving and entering by Charnley Street. Guards of these specials remained with the trains and were held responsible for them, indicating the movements necessary to the driver, from the Yard Inspector. Loose points in the yard were to be scotched, and red lights affixed to the buffer stops of all sidings. Drivers of trains using the E.L. Yard were required to give a special whistle (two whistles and a crow) to the signalman on duty at Preston Junction.

There was a set pattern of platform use after 5.00pm each day, as follows:

No.1. Trains for P.& W. Line.
No.2. All Up special trains to Chorley, Bolton and Manchester, and ordinary trains wherever possible.
No.5. Trains for L.& C. Line.
No.6. Trains for Wigan and South, Liverpool (Lime Street) and Manchester (Exchange).

Stations between Preston and Bolton, Preston and Liverpool, Preston and Southport, and Preston and Blackpool inclusive were instructed to remain open daily until assured by Control Office that no additional trains were being run.

Special empty carriage trains had to have a punctual start from the stabling point and take their turn with ordinary trains in order to ensure arrival at Preston in time to take up their scheduled workings.

Details of additional and altered passenger trains for Division "A" are not included in this publication but it must be assumed that the increase in passenger traffic was comparable with the Division "B" workings off the ex L&Y lines. Traffic was heaviest on Wednesday 6th September, which was the opening day of the Royal Lancashire Agricultural Show, and Saturday which was the culmination of the events, with a pageant. Sunday 3rd September saw comparatively few extra workings - six in all, of which train No.4. was the 7.35am ordinary working from Burnley to Blackburn extended to Preston. This comprised 6 bogies, Lower Darwen shed providing the power and train crew. No.1 was an advertised special train from Blackpool (Central) to Preston which returned at 1.15pm. No.2. worked from Blackpool as a regular service train, and worked back as an extra, departing Preston at 9.15pm to Kirkham, where it took up the 9.32pm ordinary service working to Blackpool Central. No.3. was in fact three round trips between Bolton and Preston, stock comprised 6 bogies with Bolton power the men. Train 5 worked the 1.25pm from Accrington at 1.25pm returning from Preston at 2.45pm. It next worked the 4.35pm to Preston, returning as far as Blackburn at 5.55pm. It next worked as empty stock back to Preston at 6.55pm and formed the 8.40pm to Accrington. Six bogies, engine and men were provided by Accrington. Train No.6 worked two trips from Ormskirk at 8.50am returning from Preston at 1.15pm, and again departing Ormskirk at 5.25pm and Preston at 8.04pm.

The following day (Monday 4th September) saw a significant increase with alterations to ordinary train workings from Blackpool (Central and Talbot Road), Burnley, Manchester and Todmorden. The format showed

Departure and intermediate pick-up points, arrival and departure time at Preston, stating the platform used, and dispersal point for stock. Each column is headed with the train number, together with other information such as Manchester (Victoria) departure platform, and where relevant fast or slow lines used. Time tables extend between Manchester Victoria and Blackpool, Halifax and Rose Grove, Rose Grove and Southport. Train numbers extend from 1 to 37.

After the timing pages are the carriage workings, which coincide with the train reporting numbers. For example carriage set No.1 worked the following circuit as outlined below. On Tuesday it worked circuit No.3 which commenced at Blackpool. On Wednesday it worked circuit No.5. On Thursday it worked circuit No.2. On Friday it worked circuit 5 and on Saturday it worked circuit 14.

There were some differences in the train working on different days despite what was printed in the booklet. For example, on Monday Tuesday, Friday and Saturday, Carriage Circuit 5 started with the 9.25am Blackpool (T.R.) to Preston, but on Wednesday and Thursday, this working started from Horwich at 7.13am. and had additional work into the evening finishing at Horwich on both days.

Circuit Working commencing Monday

Diagram	Start From	Loco	Finish	Due	Next day Work					
					M	T	W	Th	F	S
No. 1.	8.10am Horwich	Bolton	Blackpool C.	12.55am		3	5	2	5	14
No. 2.	8.10am Kearsley Jn.	Bolton	Blackpool T.R.	10.57pm		5	10	5	1	1
No. 3.	8.35am Blackpool C.	Blackpool	Moses Gate	1.00am		4	6	1		
No. 4.	11.05am Moses Gate	Bolton	Moses Gate	3.30pm		9	4	20	14	3
No. 5.	9.25am Blackpool C.	Blackpool. T.R.	Moses Gate	3.30pm		14	9	3	2	5
No. 6.	7.20am Moses Gate	Bolton	Kearsley	9.00pm		2	7	4	20	6
No. 7.	6.20am Blackpool T.R.	Blackpool. T.R.	Kearsley	8.40pm		-	-			
No. 8.	8.00am Manchester	Newton Heath	Manchester	10.37pm		8	8	8	8	8
No. 9.	8.55am Moses Gate	Bolton	Moses Gate	10.00pm		6	1	14	3	
No.10.	9.40am Moses Gate	Bolton	Moses Gate	11.40pm		10*	3	6	4	9
No.11	10.35am Manchester	Blackpool	then booked circuit work							
No.12.	7.10am Preston	Blackpool C.	then booked circuit work				[WThO]			
No.13.	7.47am Fleetwood	Fleetwood	then booked circuit work				[WThO]			
No.14.	3.00pm Moses Gate	Bolton	Blackpool C.	9.31pm			14	9	6	2
No.15.	7.07pm Manchester	Blackpool C.	then booked circuit work							
No.16.	8.15pm Manchester		(Service train retimed)							
No.17.	8.15pm Manchester		(Service train retimed)							
No.18.	8.15pm Manchester		(Service train retimed)							
No.19.	7.35pm Blackpool C.	Blackpool C.	Horwich	11.00pm		1	2	7	9	4
No.20.	10.00pm Blackpool T.R.	Blackpool T.R.	Moses Gate	11.40pm		10*	see 10 above			
No.21.	10.05am Rose Grove	Accrington	Rose Grove	1.15am		27	21	27	32	25
No.22.	6.00am Harwood Jn.	Accrington	Rose Grove	10.30pm		-	-	32	25	32
No.23.	6.15am Ormskirk	Ormskirk	then booked circuit work							
No.24.	8.50am Ormskirk	Ormskirk	Rose Grove	11.15pm		21	27	14	3	
No.25.	11.45am Gisburn	Lower Darwen	Rose Grove	9.50pm		32	22	32	25	32
No.26.	6.20am Colne	Colne	Harwood Jn.	9.40pm		-	-	25	-	35
No.27.	6.50am Rose Grove	Accrington	Ormskirk	8.40pm		24	24	24	21	27
No.28.	9.15am Southport	Southport	Southport	12.40am		28	28	28	28	28
No.29.	7.00am Gisburn	Lower Darwen	Gisburn	10.42pm		29	29	29	29	29
No.30.	7.55am Ormskirk	Ormskirk	Ormskirk	10.45pm		30	30	30	30	30
No.31.	8.27am Blackburn	Lower Darwen	Blackburn	9.42am	then booked circuit work					
No.32.	7.55am Rose Grove	Rose Grove	Gisburn	12.20am		25	26	25	-	35
No.33.	9.35am Blackburn	Lower Darwen	Blackburn	10.37am	then booked circuit work					
No.34.	7.10am Low Moor	Low Moor	Low Moor.	9.30pm		34	34	34	34	34
No.35.	12.35pm Nelson M.Yd.[SO]	Colne	Nelson M.Y.	10.58pm		-	-	-	-	
No.36.	6.00pm Ormskirk	Ormskirk	Ormskirk	12.25am		36	36	36	36	36
No.37.	9.45pm Blackpool T.R.	Blackpool T.R.	Preston	11.21pm	—	37	37	37	37	37
			Daily booked workings:		31	31	37	37	30	31

Circuits 1-10, 14, 19 comprised 15 coaches. Circuits 11 and 15 comprised 8 bogies, Circuits 20 comprised 10 carriages, Circuits 21,24,25,27,29 and 32 comprised 14 carriages, Circuits 28,30,31,33 and 36 comprised 6 bogies. The remainder were unspecified and arranged locally. Additional operating clauses were:

Nos 38 & 39. Two engines to be at Preston E.L. 8.00am to work as required to avoid engines of special trains arriving in the Goods Yard or Station having to run round their train.

No.40. An engine to be at Preston E.L. 6.00am to shunt as required throughout the day.

No.41. Additional guards at Preston E.L.

      No.1. at 8.00am to work as required.

      No.2. at 5.00pm to work as required.

No.42. This clause covered variations to the regular service train coach diagrams. It covered workings to and from Preston from and to most stations within the Operating Area.

Sequence of Circuit Diagrams

No.1. - Monday

Engine leaves Bolton Shed 7.40am

15 carriages.

arr		dep	
...	Horwich	8.10am	
8.54am	Preston	8.58	ECS
9.35	Blackpool (C)	5.00pm	ECS
5.30pm	Preston	5.35	
5.55	Chorley	6.45	ECS
7.10	Preston	7.15	
7.52	Blackpool (T.R.)	9.15	ECS
9.50	Preston	9.55	
10.17	Chorley	11.20	ECS
11.40	Preston	12.00mn	
12.55am	Blackpool (C)		

Works No.3. Tuesday.

No.3. - Tuesday

Engine leaves Blackpool (C) Shed 8.05am

15 carriages

arr		dep	
...	Blackpool (C)	8.35am	
9.26am	Preston	9.30	ECS
9.50	Chorley	10.43	
11.05	Preston	11.10	ECS
11.50	Blackpool (T.R.)	7.10pm	ECS
7.41pm	Preston	7.45	
8.02	Chorley	8.40	ECS
9.00	Preston	9.05	
9.48	Blackpool (T.R.)	10.55	ECS
12.05am	Horwich		

Works No.5. Wednesday

No.5. - Wednesday

Engine leaves Horwich Shed at 6.40am

15 carriages

arr		dep	
...	Horwich	7.13am	
7.48am	Preston	7.52	ECS
8.30	Blackpool (T.R.)	9.25	
10.13	Preston	10.16	ECS
11.00	Bolton via Lostock Hall Jn.	12.25pm	
1.05pm	Preston	1.12	ECS
1.42	Blackpool (T.R.)	5.40	ECS
6.17	Preston	6.20	
6.37	Chorley	7.25	ECS
7.50	Preston	7.55	
8.26	Blackpool (C)	8.55	ECS
9.35	Preston	9.45	
10.02	Chorley	10.05	ECS
10.20	Horwich		

Works No.2. Thursday

No.2. - Thursday

Engine leaves Horwich Shed at 5.30am

arr		dep	
...	Horwich	5.55am	
6.30am	Preston	6.40	ECS
7.12	Bolton	8.30	
9.19	Preston	9.23	ECS
10.00	Blackpool (C)	10.50	
11.47	Preston	11.53	ECS
12.36pm	Bolton	1.50pm	
2.32	Preston	2.37	ECS
3.18	Blackpool (T.R.)	5.55	ECS
6.26	Preston	6.30	
7.12	Bolton	9.35	ECS
10.15	Preston	10.20	
10.57	Blackpool (T.R.)		

Works No.5. Friday

No.5. - Friday

Engine leaves Blackpool (T.R.) Shed at 8.55am

arr		dep	
...	Blackpool (T.R.)	9.25am	
10.13am	Preston	10.16	ECS
11.00	Bolton	12.25pm	
1.05pm	Preston	1.12	ECS
1.42	Blackpool (T.R.) [with 4]	2.00	ECS
3.30	Moses Gate		

Works No.14 Saturday.

No.14. - Saturday

Engine leaves Bolton Shed at 2.30pm

arr		dep	
...	Moses Gate	3.00pm	ECS
3.40pm	Ribble Sidings	4.50	ECS
4.55	Preston	5.00	
5.50	Blackpool (C)	6.22	ECS
6.50	Preston	6.55	
7.35	Horwich	7.50	ECS
8.33	Preston	8.40	
9.31	Blackpool (C)		

The working of Preston station was complex enough without the extra excursion traffic generated. Most of these extra trains running had on average, five minutes at the platform to load or discharge before moving off. Taking Wednesday September 6th as the busiest, it is worth while looking at the time tables, extracted from the relevant pages of the booklet.

Bolton, Manchester to Preston. Disposal normally to Blackpool (Talbot Road or Central). Hor.=Horwich, Bolt.=Bolton.

Train No.		1	2	3	14	4	5	6	1	7	2	8	9	10	3	11	4
Preston	arr	6.15	6.30	6.52	7.10	7.36	7.48	8.25	8.54	9.00	9.18	9.33	9.53	10.33	11.05	11.28	12.00
platform		3	1	1	4	1	1	1	1	1	1	1	1	1	1	1	1
Preston	dep	6.25	6.40	6.55	7.15	7.40	7.52	8.30	8.58	9.05	9.23	9.37	9.58	10.38	11.10	11.30	12.05
to Blackpool		Hor.	Bolt.	Cent.	Cent.	TRd	TRd	Cent.		Cent.	Cent.	Cent.	T.Rd	Cent.	T.Rd.	T.Rd	T.Rd

Train No.		5	2	10	14	9	1	5	15	14	3	2	19	1
Preston	arr	1.05	2.32	4.11	4.55	6.00	7.10	7.50	8.10	8.33	9.00	10.15	11.30	11.40
platform		1	1	1	1	1	1	1	1	1	1	1	1	1
Preston	dep	1.12	2.37	4.15	5.00	6.03	7.15	7.55	8.13	8.40	9.10	10.20	-	12.00
to Blackpool		T.Rd	T.Rd	T.Rd	Cent.	Cent.	T.Rd	Cent.	Cent.	Cent.	T.Rd.	T.Rd.	E/L	Cent.

****

Train No		1	2	7	9	12	12	3	4	14	5	2	10	9	1	5	2
Preston	arr	-	-	7.05	7.17	7.58	8.35	9.26	9.35	10.10	10.13	11.47	1.45	2.10	5.30	6.17	6.26
platform		2	2	7	6	2	9	2	2	2	6	6	10	6	2	2	2
Preston	dep	6.25	6.40	7.10	7.20	8.12	8.38	9.30	9.40	10.13	10.16	11.53	1.50	2.12	5.35	6.20	6.30
to		Hor.	Bolt	Chor	Bolt	M/c.	Kirk	Chor	Bolt	R.S.	Bolt	Bolt	Bolt.	R.S.	Chor.	Chor.	Bolt.

Train No.		14	7	3	6	19	9	8	5	1	10	37	20	3
Preston	arr	6.50	7.20	7.41	7.50	8.20	8.57	9.15	9.35	9.50	10.10	10.15	10.37	11.40
platform		2	2	2	2	2	2	2	2	2	2	2	2	2
Preston	dep	6.55	7.30	7.45	8.00	8.25	9.03	9.27	9.45	9.55	10.20	10.25	10.42	12.00
to		Hor.	Kear	Chor	Kear	M/c.	Moses	M/c.	Hor.	Chor.	Hor.	H.B.	Moses	Moses

Destinations:
Hor.=Horwich, Bolt.=Bolton, Chor.=Chorley, M/c.=Manchester, Kirk.=Kirkham, R.S.=Ribble Sidings, Kear=Kearsley, Moses=Moses Gate, H.B.=Hesketh Bank.

*****

Trains terminating in Preston Goods Yard, or station:

Train No.		21	22	23	24	25	26	27	21	28	29	30	31	32	24	28	33
from		Bbm	M.H.	Orm.	R.G.	H.J.	Cne.	R.G.	M.H.	Spt.	Gis.	Orm.	Bbm	R.G.	Orm.	Spt.	Tod.
Preston sta.	arr	-	-	6.55	-	-	-	-	-	8.10	-	8.35	-	-	9.31	9.58	-
Preston G.Y.	arr	6.23	6.40	-	7.00	7.16	7.37	7.54	8.06	-	8.26	-	8.52	9.03	-	-	10.04
Preston G.Y.	dep	6.32	6.50	-	7.20	7.30	7.50	8.05	8.19	-	8.40	-	9.20	-	-	-	10.15
Preston sta.	dep	-	-	7.10	-	-	-	-	-	8.26	-	8.45	-	-	9.40	10.10	-
Disposal to		M.H.	G.H.	Orm.	Orm.	Gis.	H.J.	H.J.	R.G.	Spt.	H.J.	Orm.	Bbm	-	Acc.	H.B.	Bbm.

Train No.		33	34	21	30	28	24	25	28	30	21	26	25
from		Tod.	Hfx.	R.G.	Orm.	H.B.	Acc.	Gis.	Spt.	Orm.	R.G.	H.J.	H.J.
Preston sta.	arr	-	-	-	11.40	11.51	-	-	2.13	-	-	-	-
Preston G.Y.	arr	10.04	10.08	11.12	-	-	12.52	1.25	-	2.20	2.56	3.50	7.09
Preston G.Y.	dep	10.15	-	11.26	-	-	-	-	-	-	-	-	-
Preston sta.	dep	-	-	-	12.00	12.10	-	-	-	-	-	-	-
Disposal to		Bbm	-	R.G.	Orm.	Spt.	-	-	-	-	-	-	-

Trains Departing Preston Goods Yard (Charnley Street) or Butler Street:

Train No.	21	25	24	26	28	21	25	30	32	24	36	28	26	34	25	30
From store at	-	-	-	-	-	H.J.	H.J.	-	-	-	Acc.	H.B.	H.J.	-	-	Orm.
Preston B.S. arr	-	-	-	-	-	-	-	-	-	6.10	6.30	6.45	-	-	-	7.20
Preston G.Y. arr	-	-	-	-	-	4.30	5.00	-	-	-	-	-	6.55	-	-	-
Preston G.Y. dep	3.15	3.30	4.15	4.27	-	5.05	5.18	-	5.47	6.30	-	-	7.12	7.30	7.40	-
Preston B.S. dep	-	-	-	-	4.55	-	-	5.30	-	-	6.45	7.02	-	-	-	7.50
To	H.J.	H.J.	Acc.	H.J.	H.B.	Bly.	H.J.	Orm.	H.J.	Gis.	Orm.	Spt.	H.J.	Hfx.	Cne.	Orm.

Train No.	32	21	36	26	29	28	22	24	30	37	32	36	28	21	37
From store at	H.J.	Bly.	Orm.	H.J.	H.J.	Spt.	G.H.	Gis.	Orm.	-	H.J.	Lpl.	Spt.	Acc.	H.B.
Preston B.S. arr	-	-	8.45	-	-	9.02	-	-	9.30	-	-	11.30	11.14	10.55	11.21
Preston G.Y. arr	7.45	8.15	-	8.30	8.50	-	9.25	9.36	-	-	10.32	-	-	-	-
Preston G.Y. dep	8.05	8.55	-	9.05	9.25	-	9.45	10.00	-	-	10.50	-	-	-	-
Preston B.S. dep	-	-	9.00	-	-	9.25	-	-	10.05	10.25	-	11.45	11.50	12.00	-
To	H.J.	Acc.	Lpl.	H.J.	Gis.	Spt.	R.G.	R.G.	Orm.	H.B.	H.J.	Orm.	Spt.	R.G.	-

Abbreviations:
Bburn=Blackburn, M.H.=Mill Hill, G.H.=Great Harwood, Orm.=Ormskirk, R.G.=Rose Grove, H.J.=Harwood Junction, Gis.=Gisburn, Cne.=Colne, Spt.=Southport, Acc.=Accrington, H.B.=Hesketh Bank, Tod.=Todmorden, Hfx.=Halifax, Bly.=Burnley, Lpl.=Liverpool via Ormskirk.

The final section of the book outlines the Staff Arrangements. The period of coverage is extended slightly - from August 28th to September 16th inclusive, and specifies the duties of named personnel. For example, Clerk T.H. Powell is assigned to take duty in the Staff Office and assist generally as required. Station Inspector T.Storey is charged on September 3rd, to see that the arrangements for the following Monday are complete. Relief Clerks - Messrs. A.J.H. Turner, J. Sumner, H. Vernon, C. Rolfe, D. Unsworth, R. Smith, J. Jones and W. Curwen are given specific working points and hours of duty in the booking offices - the first four in the North Union and the remainder in the E.L. office.

Additional telegraph office staff comprised Messrs R.W.B. Lindsay, M. Hughes (Wigan), McCrossan (Manchester "A", A.C.B. Mercer and H. Speakman, (Lime Street), and W.Smith, M. Wood. Additional Telegraph Messengers were Messrs R. Chadwick, W. Nuttall and W. Balshaw.

Platforms were provided with additional staff, some brought in for the week from other stations. Supervising platforms 1 and 2 were Station Inspector W.Green (Bolton "B") and Yard Foreman M. Sumner, upgraded to Inspector for the 7.0am to 3.00pm shift, with Station Inspector R.W. Morley of Warrington assisted by Inspector W. Moxton on the afternoon turn from 3.00pm until 11.00pm. On Nos 6 and 7 platforms, Station Inspector J. Kell covered the morning shift and Station Inspector E. Peasley from Wigan worked the late turn.

Platform duties with specific responsibilities for directing passengers were given to porters W.H. Wheeler (early turn) and S.P. Miller (late turn), both from Warrington and assigned to work on platform 1 and 2. Porter J.H. Lawless of Warrington supervised on platforms 3 and 4 on afternoon turn. Porters transferred from Edge Hill were allocated work on the afternoon turn as follows: H.D. Stewart on No.5 platform, A.C. Beattie on No.6 platform, W. King on No.7 platform, J.H. Tatham on Nos 1 & 2 platforms, and L. Huttley on No.6 platform. Porter J. Kilshaw of Huyton assisted on No.5 platform. J.McDermott was a junior Telephone Attendant based on platform 6 working the afternoon turn, whilst porter J. Bowdell worked a late turn with specific responsibility to attend to engine headboards and indicator.

Other duties were specified, too numerous to mention individually, but these covered manning the ticket barriers, the excess luggage department, cloakroom, the station and parcel offices and lavatories. Additional Railway Police were located at strategic positions according to requirements.

Staff at signal boxes were strengthened by provision of train bookers and assistants to the regular signalmen at Ribble Sidings, Preston No.1 box, No.4 box, No.5 box, Whelley Junction, Haigh Junction and Roundhouse. Additional passenger traffic staff were required for a variety of duties at Butler Street and at the (E.L.) Goods Yard. At Oxheys yard, which was used to store passenger vehicles, the yard staff were designated alternative work to their normal duties.

At the Show Ground (Moor Park), an enquiry office was established for the duration of the show, together with additional enquiry and advertising kiosks. Likewise, live stock traffic had its own booking office, with staff to man it. This affected the yards at Bamber Bridge, Blackburn (Taylor Street), Midge Hall, Lostock Hall, Leyland, Lea Road, Kirkham and Roundhouse.

Finally, the event affected station workings outside the immediate Preston station limits, and the Lancaster & Carlisle District required alterations to the hours of duty of staff at Barton and Broughton, Brock, Garstang and Catterall, Scorton, Bay Horse, Galgate and Lancaster. The Ingleton Branch was similarly affected and altered staff duties were specified for Sedbergh, Barbon, Kirkby Lonsdale, Ingleton (LNW) and Ingleton (Midland). Other stations affected were Bare Lane, Morecambe, Burneside, Staveley and Windermere.

1952

Mr. R. G. Ellis, Preston Station Master, shows the Magazine reporter the bell which rang the "all aboard" signal when Anglo-Scottish expresses used to stop for 20 minutes at the station while passengers dined in the refreshment room. The clock on the wall, marked "N.U. No. 6" is believed to date from about 1838

The Magazine Roving Reporter visits:—

Preston

Looking for anyone on Preston station can be a trifle confusing if your railway history is rusty. As a railwayman you are quite likely to be told (as I was) "Oh he's over on the N.U. side." If you counter this (as I did) with a vacant look, your informant is likely to add the explanation "The L.N.W.R. side" and accompany it with an unmistakable nod in the direction of the westerly side of the station.

Supposing the man you were looking for had gone to the other side of the station? In that case you might be told he was on the E.L. or L.Y.R. side. All of which harks back to the days when there were two stations in one at Preston.

The N.U. side is so called because it was originally the North Union Railway station, the North Union being the title adopted by the infant Preston & Wigan Railway and the Wigan Branch Railway when they combined in 1834. In 1888 after many developments and working agreements with other lines the N.U. was absorbed jointly by the L.N.W.R. and the L.Y.R. This joint station became locally known as the "L.N.W.R."

The East Lancashire side of the station gets its name from the E.L.R. station which was opened there in 1850. In 1859 the E.L.R. amalgamated with the L.Y.R. and its station became entirely L.Y.R. property.

In 1923 both the L.Y.R.—L.N.W.R. Joint station and the L.Y.R. station became part of the L.M.S. and the duplication of staff—there were, among other things, two station masters—became unnecessary. The two stations, being side by side and physically joined so that they were ostensibly one station, this process of combination was a simple one.

The North Union side of today's station, one of the largest on the London Midland, covers the adjacent Christian

Road goods station, the horse dock, the up and down through lines and platforms 1 to 7 (including bays 5 and 6). The East Lancs. side of the station consists of platforms 8, 9 and 10, bays 11, 12 and 13,

the fish dock with Butler Street goods station adjoining.

Two sets of entrance buildings standing side by side are connected by an overbridge with access to all platforms. The station's main stem is the island platform (Nos. 5 and 6) built in 1880 which is 1253 feet long. This is the nerve centre of the station and in its backbone of three-storey brick buildings are housed the Preston District Operating Superintendent and his staff, the district control room, the Station Master's office, the enquiry bureau, the Inspector's room known far and wide as "No. 20" because of its telephone extension number, the train announcer's room, the G.P.O. parcels and letter sorting rooms and the main refreshment rooms. A continuously open staff snack bar is a recent and much frequented addition.

I started my tour of the station in the office of Mr. C. J. Vidal the D.O.S. where I met Mr. W. F. P. Thompson the Asst. D.O.S. who told me something of

Preston's operating problems. district's northermost point on the line is Penrith from which it ex southwards to Euxton (pronounced E Junction. Blackpool and Fleetwoo the westerly limits and Bamber B and Lostock Hall the easterly. Ther also branch lines to Keswick, Winderr Ingleton and Morecambe. The di covers 218 route miles (including 77 of main line, the longest stretch on London Midland operating district) trolled through 143 signalboxes.

Passenger traffic is heavy, espe during summer for, in addition to be "half-way house" mid-way between ton and Glasgow and much used a interchange station, Preston is the junction between all other lines Blackpool and serves locally the la centre of population (120,000) of single station. Furthermore, Prest the obvious place for trains from East West Lancashire to connect with ser to and from the North.

Normal summer passenger traffi Preston amounts to more than 350 up down trains daily (25 approximatel each direction do not stop), but there wide variation in these figures. Saturdays, for instance, about additional trains use the station calling, 193 passing) which swells daily total to nearly 700. With spe and excursions, Preston's Saturday f for passenger trains sometimes approa 1,000 and this is exclusive of empty s trains. The so-called "cotton holid when whole towns close their works thousands of their employees go holiday at the same time cause seas rushes of traffic between many north towns and Blackpool all of which pa through Preston.

Such heavy programmes of passe trains affect, of course, the freight gramme which involves the moveme some 200 and more trains a day. M of the freight movement from Presto concerned with short trips to and f nearby centres and marshalling po Preston itself being too busy and ha insufficient accommodation for the ma up of numerous complete trains. Butler Street goods station receives forwards freight to Lostock Hall

Preston parcels office deals with a wide variety of traffic—this item was a crate of luggage destined for an army sergeant in Khartoum. Left to right are Messrs. R. Tye, R. Crook, C. Davidson and J. Dolan

Plan showing Preston's main line and l rail connections

...two sets of station buildings may be seen right and left in this photograph. Both ...dings have approach roads leading down to them. The East Lancs. side of the station ... the left and the North Union side on the right in the picture

"Pramming" goods from warehouse to rail vans at the Christian Road Depot under the supervision of Foreman Mr. A. C. Nicol

...gton and the Christian Road depot ...t traffic is dealt with through ...gton, Ribble sidings and North ...n sidings.

...e Preston Corporation Dock which ...prises 2-3 miles of berths is served by ...gle line which branches off from the ... side of the station and disappears ...a 1 in 30 gradient into a tunnel. It ...crosses the main Liverpool— ...kpool road by means of an un-gated ...crossing. Coal and general merchan- ...mainly for Northern Irish ports is ...n to the docks and imports of wood ...esparto grass, china clay, petrol and ...tock are brought away. About 2,500 ...ns move in each direction every week ...this busy single line, no fewer than ...wagons daily being used to deliver ...to the Preston power station situated ...he dockside. Twelve trips a day are ...e in each direction between Preston ...on and the docks and this work is ...ed out by three engines (class 7 F's) ...one is kept in readiness as a banker. ...t of the coal delivered comes from ...kshire and the East Midlands.

...here are twenty signal boxes under the ...rol of the Preston station master but ...hese only five, with an aggregate of ...e 500 levers are concerned with train ...ements in and through the station. ...busiest of these is Preston No. 4 ...ch had a new frame installed in 1948 ...deals with a daily average of 600 ...s of all types. The box has 168 ...king levers, 15 telephones, 18 block ...ruments, 8 route indicators and 6 ...icle on line" indicators. Three ...ninated diagrams assist the signalmen ...means of track circuits. No workable ...nt signals are controlled from ...ton No. 4 there being a speed limit of ...n.p.h. on all main lines through the ...on and all distant signals for approach- ...trains are fixed in the "caution" ...tion. Box No. 4 is situated at the ...h end of the station between the ...n and up main lines and is staffed by ...gnalmen and a lad on early and late ...s and two signalmen and a lad on ...ts.

...ly next call was at the station master's ...e where I met Mr. R. G. Ellis, the ...ion Master, formally attired in the ...ventional dress of a "Top Hat" ...on master, seated at a huge executive- ...d desk going through the morning's ... with Mr. G. Johnson his chief clerk.

...r. Ellis has a staff of 350 to help him ...the station. This total includes three ...stant station masters, 17 inspectors, ...foremen, 7 clerks, 90 signalmen, 50 ...ers, 20 shunters, 25 ticket collectors ...50 parcel porters. Every man on the ...ion has an important job to do. ...ing the morning and evening residen- ...rush hours when platform and line ...pation is heavy the regulation of ...ns through the station becomes an

intricate task and it is sometimes necessary to replatform trains. This is never done unless absolutely necessary as it may inconvenience the public and complicate the task of the signalmen, but, should it occur, passengers are told by means of the station public address system which constantly broadcasts train information. In fact, to the visitor it seems that the train announcer is hardly ever "off the air" such is the intensity of services at certain times. Adjacent to the Station Master's office and immediately facing the entrance to the main island platform is the station enquiry bureau, glass fronted and with a full-length counter inside, where passenger's queries are dealt with by a specially-trained staff.

Preston, as a town, is strong in civic

Mr. James Beardsworth, Cartage Foreman at the Christian Road goods depot, discusses a point with Number Taker Mr. G. Simpson

pride and is well known as "Proud Preston." Evidence of this pride was pointed out to me by Mr. Ellis in the form of a brass plaque commemorating the Preston Free Buffet for Servicemen which during the 1914-18 war served more than three million cups of tea and other refreshments to soldier and sailor travel- lers. This generous idea was carried on in an even bigger way during the recent war when more than eight million travelling servicemen were given free refreshments at Preston.

In Mr. Ellis's office there are two interesting relics of Preston railway history. One is the clock which is marked "N.U. No. 6" and would seem to date from the earliest days of the North Union Railway (circa 1838) and the other is a brass handbell. The bell is one of two which used to be rung to warn diners in the refreshment room that their train was about to depart. This was a very necessary warning for from 1863 onwards, up and down Anglo-Scottish expresses used to

stop at Preston at the same time for 20 minutes each while the passengers lunched in the refreshment room. "Twenty minutes to dine" was the cry which greeted travellers as the trains slowed down to a stop, and the ringing of the bells, one on platform 5 and the other on 6, used to warn them that it was time to be on the way again. Such arrangements went out with the introduction of rest- aurant cars and today the Scottish expresses except those to and from Manchester and Liverpool pass through without stopping.

The second bell, so I was told, was "borrowed" by some Preston football fans to instil a little urgency into a local team. It was never returned and Mr. Ellis is taking good care that the remaining bell does not go the way of its twin.

Two of the blocks of buildings on the main island platform are occupied by the Post Office and used as letter and parcels post sorting and forwarding offices and stores. The sorting is done mostly at night, parcels and letters being brought in and sorted for immediate loading on to trains, thus dispensing with the need for motor vans to carry sorted mail from the town G.P.O. to the station. Here on Preston station more than 2½ million letters and 70 thousand postal parcels are sorted and forwarded every week.

The station has its own parcels side of course and this is centred on the parcels office on the East Lancs. side of the station. Road vans working from 3.30 a.m. to 7.0 p.m. load up and unload at the parcels deck which forms one side of the glass-roofed office. The parcels staff (12 clerks, 7 vanmen, 4 lads, 4 office porters and junior porters) claim that they deal with some of the most diverse traffic of any similar office on the Region. Day old chicks are forwarded at the rate of about 400 boxes a week; they are packed 20 to a box and are noisy for their age, their vigorous cheeps providing a sibilant background to the other noises of the office. Quite a few calves are handled too, as many as 70 a day on some market days (Tuesdays). Mostly they are consigned to Scotland and in large numbers they are loaded at the Christian Road horse dock on the other side of the station.

One unusual consignment was a 4½ cwt. prize ram; he was made quite at home in the parcels office with some pedigree pigs individually crated. At the time of my visit the parcels staff were arranging for two special trains to convey 30 horses, personnel and baggage of the Lancashire County Constabulary to Peterborough and Kelso, Scotland, where they are to give displays at agri- cultural shows.

In charge of the parcels office is Mr. F. Martin the Preston Passenger and Parcels Agent who is also concerned with all the booking offices on the station. Mr. J. G. Swarbrick is the parcels office senior clerk.

The goods side of Preston station working is the domain of Mr. T. Grimes the Goods Agent. He controls both the Butler Street depot, which deals with all full load traffic and sundries traffic for East Lancashire and the North East, and the Christian Road depot which handles sundries traffic for all parts of the country other than that dealt with by Butler Street.

In addition to these two main depots, both modernised in 1938, there are five others under his control. Preston, having a docks, is a port in its own right and through it more than a million tons of traffic passed out of the country last year, much of it being dealt with by rail access.

The Goods Agent's staff, headed by Mr. John Wray the Chief Clerk who has been at Preston 40 years and Chief Foreman Mr. T. J. W. Cousins, includes 73 clerks, 9 supervisors, and 220 concilia- tion grades. In a typical four weekly period they deal with 20,940 tons (8,328 wagon loads) of general merchandise, 94,466 tons (9,169 wagons) of coal and coke and 5,718 tons (654 wagons) of mineral traffic.

Preston is a zonal centre and delivers sundries traffic over an area of about 200 square miles, to perform which (together with full load traffic for the immediate area of Preston town) a fleet of 32 motors and 18 horses is maintained at Christian Road and Butler Street depots. In addition, a stud of 29 horses is employed on internal station duties which comprise mainly the cartage of sundries traffic unloaded from wagons received at Preston which is transhipped and sent forward by rail.

The industrial strength of Preston springs mainly from cotton weaving, rayon spinning and electrical and other types of engineering. The town has always been in the forefront of industry and trade in the North West and as long ago as 1328 the Guild Merchants of Pres- ton had organised themselves into trade fraternities of a sort. These included clockmakers, cordwainers, cow leeches or farriers and flax dressers. Every twenty years these organisations held a "guild" or week of celebration during which religious and trade processions and civic functions were arranged. These guild weeks are still carried on and, as the 1942 one was not held owing to the war, it is being celebrated this year from 1st-6th September. The Preston Guild gives local pride full scope for expression and during my visit posters bearing the Preston coat of arms were everywhere advertising the Preston Guild.

STATION CLOSURES

	Passengers		Goods	
Barton & Broughton	1 May	1939	31 May	1965
Brock	1 May	1939	5 April	1954
Butler Street goods	—		29 Nov	1971
Christian Road goods	—		29 Nov	1971
Corporation Street & Dock Street coal yards	—		11 Nov	1968
Deepdale Street (P&LR terminus)	1 Nov	1856	open	
Deepdale (Road)	2 June	1930	no goods	
Farington	7 Mar	1960	7 Mar	1960
Greenbank Sidings goods	—		1 Feb	1966
Grimsargh	2 June	1930	6 Nov	1967
Lea Road	2 May	1938	no goods	
Longridge	2 June	1930	16 Oct	1967
Longton Bridge	7 Sept	1964	6 Apr	1964
Lostock Hall	7 Aug	1968	25 Jan	1965
(reopened to passengers only, 14 May 1984)				
Maudland Bridge	1 June	1885	no goods	
Maudlands (P&WR — later goods station)	11 Apr	1844	July	1981
Maxwell House	11 Apr	1844	no goods	
Midge Hall	2 Oct	1961	2 Oct	1961
New Longton & Hutton	7 Sept	1964	no goods	
Oxheys cattle sidings	28 Feb	1925	9 Sept	1968
Penwortham Cop Lane	7 Sept	1964	no goods	
Ribbleton (formerly Fulwood, originally Gammer Lane)	2 June	1930	no goods	
Ribbleton (near Fulwood Barracks)		1866	no goods	
Todd Lane Junction (formerly Preston Junction)	1 May	1972	no goods	
West Lancashire station (Fishergate Hill)	16 July	1900	25 Jan	1965

LINE CLOSURES

	Passengers		Goods	
Longridge Branch	2 June	1930	see below	
Courtaulds' Siding to Longridge	—		16 Oct	1967
Deepdale Junction (500yd east) to Courtaulds' Siding	—		2 Aug	1980
Whittingham Hospital Railway	29 June	1957	29 June	1957
East Lancashire lines				
Farington, original Blackburn & Preston Ry curve, east-to-north	2 Sept	1850	2 Sept	1850
Preston to Bamber Bridge and Lostock Hall Junctions	1 May	1972	1 May	1972
Lostock Hall Engine Shed Junction to Moss Lane Junction	6 Oct	1969	1 May	1972
West Lancashire Railway				
Ribble Junction to Middleforth Junction	16 July	1900	16 July	1900
Penwortham Junction to Fishergate Hill	16 July	1900	7 Sept	1964
Remainder	7 Sept	1964	7 Sept	1964

Other Sources of Reference

The Lancaster Canal Tramroad, by Gordon Biddle, *Journal* of the Railway & Canal Historical Society, Vol. IX, Nos. 5 & 6, 1963.

Chronology of the Railways of Lancashire, by M D Greville (Railway & Canal Historical Society, 1973)

Register of Closed Passenger Stations & Goods Depots in England, Scotland & Wales, C R Clinker (Avon Anglia, 1971)

A Regional History of the Railways of Great Britain: Vol 10, The North West, 2nd Edn, G O Holt (David & Charles, 1978)

The Lancashire & Yorkshire Railway, 3 Vols, John Marshall (David & Charles, 1969)

The Preston & Longridge Railway, Norman Parker (Oakwood Press, 1972)

The East Lancashire Railway, R W Rush (Oakwood Press, 1983)

The West Lancashire Railway, J E Cotterall (Oakwood Press, 1982)

Over Shap to Carlisle, Harold D Bowtell (Ian Allan, 1983)

The Railway Magazine:
Vol XII, 1903, *Notable Railway Stations, No 20, Preston,* J L Lawrence
Vol LVIII, 1926, *Notable Railway Stations & their Traffic, Preston,* J F Gairns
Vol 103, 1957, *The Whittingham Railway,* H C Casserley
Vol 104, 1958, *Affray at Whittingham,* Norman Jones
Vol 106, 1960, *Railway Development in Preston* (three articles), M D Greville & G O Holt

I must also acknowledge the value of *Lancashire & Yorkshire Railway Historical Maps* by R A Cook (Railway & Canal Historical Society, 1974), on which the map at the front of this book is based.

Other Titles by the Author

Canals of North West England, 2 Vols, with Charles Hadfield (Canals of the British Isles series, David & Charles, 1970)

Victorian Stations: railway stations in England & Wales, 1830-1923 (David & Charles, 1973)

The British Railway Station, with Jeoffry Spence (Railway History in Pictures series, David & Charles, 1977)

Pennine Waterway: the Leeds & Liverpool Canal, (Dalesman, 2nd Edn, 1979)

Lancashire Waterways, (Dalesman, 1980)

Railway Stations in the North West, (Dalesman, 1981)

The Railway Heritage of Britain, with O S Nock and other authors (Michael Joseph, 1983)

Great Railway Stations of Britain; their architecture, growth and development, (David & Charles, 1986)